ꓵG'S LIFE
ꜰOR OTHER
THE
HALF

Tales from in and around a vet's practice

❝ Hilarious & eminently readable ❞

04270116

Steve Ankers

IT'S A
DOG'S LIFE
FOR THE OTHER
HALF

Tales from in and around a vet's practice

MEREO
Cirencester

Mereo Books

1A The Wool Market Dyer Street Cirencester Gloucestershire GL7 2PR
An imprint of Memoirs Publishing www.mereobooks.com

It's a Dog's Life for the Other Half: 978-1-86151-199-7

First published in Great Britain in 2014
by Mereo Books, an imprint of Memoirs Publishing

The address for Memoirs Publishing Group Limited can be found at
www.memoirspublishing.com

The Memoirs Publishing Group Ltd Reg. No. 7834348

The Memoirs Publishing Group supports both The Forest Stewardship Council® (FSC®) and
the PEFC® leading international forest-certification organisations. Our books carrying both the
FSC label and the PEFC® and are printed on FSC®-certified paper. FSC® is the only
forest-certification scheme supported by the leading environmental organisations including
Greenpeace. Our paper procurement policy can be found at
www.memoirspublishing.com/environment

Typeset in 12/18pt Bembo
by Wiltshire Associates Publisher Services Ltd. Printed and bound in Great Britain by
Printondemand-Worldwide, Peterborough PE2 6XD

To my wife, Margaret, my big brother, John, and all vets
everywhere who made this book necessary...

...and to Molly the Labrador, Kenny Bunny, Peanuts the antique
tom, Poppy, the true and loyal hamster, and all the other
pets they've tended and terminated.

INTRODUCTION

All Creatures — some great, some not so great, to be frank…

I grew up with the James Herriot books and their TV adaptations. To me they weren't a fictional escape, they were a documentary account of my brother John's life as a vet in rural Northumberland. On the telly you could revel in the mud and laugh in the face of the infectious diseases, but in true life those things were just, well, mud and diseases. And, while my big brother was clearly in his element — and being paid — I was normal. Normalish.

So, what happened next? I met, walked out with and married one of my brother's veterinary assistants, Margaret, and my fate was sealed. A life of night-time emergency call outs, late arrivals at social events, toe-curling conversation at friends' dinner tables, unidentifiable stains on our clothes and abandoned creatures sharing our home. What's not to like?

There have been amusing, heartwarming, harrowing and occasionally disgusting encounters with pets - and owners - of all varieties, shapes and sizes. There have been camels, vultures, wallabies and escaped alligators; dodgy greyhound trainers, macho abattoir workers, a Cliff Richard cassette tape extracted from an extraordinary place, and the cat that ate a Chihuahua.

"Write about all the things that happen. That would be interesting" suggested my wife, "and work in something about wizards."

"Wizards."

"J K Rowling wrote about wizards and people loved it."

No wizards. This is my story. And I'm sticking to it.

Steve Ankers | Summer 2014

ACKNOWLEDGMENTS

Thanks go to my brother, John Prescott – "Northumberland's longest serving vet" – to his son and veterinary partner, Sam, and all the Prescott family for Northumbrian memories and some great meals.

Mairi Ankers has played the vital roles of being the butt of many of the jibes in this book, an excellent critic of my efforts, and our daughter.

And, finally, my biggest debt of gratitude goes to my wife, Margaret, the Angel of Mercy (and occasionally of Death), who has been at the heart of many of the stories described here and came up with the original idea. Is that OK, dear?

ABOUT THE AUTHOR

Steve Ankers now works part time with a "national park friends group", the South Downs Society, following a career in the environment field in Greater Manchester and Sussex. He has co-authored two satirical books on town planning in the semi-mythical conurbation of Grotton and writes and blogs on travel and other subjects. He worries about his global footprint and Liverpool FC and no longer plays tiddlywinks to a respectable standard. Steve lives in Lewes, East Sussex, with his wife, Margaret, random pets and occasional visits from their daughter, Mairi, when she wants something.

Follow Steve at: sankersblog.wordpress.com

"A word of warning before you start to read *A Dog's Life*: prepare to do one of those marathon reads that takes you from dawn till dusk. The book is thoroughly unputdownable, unlike some of the more desperate animals featured in its pages. Filled with amusing anecdotes about life married to a vet and with a vet as a brother, Steve Ankers' book is entertaining, enthralling and totally engaging. *A Dog's Life* should be read by anyone who likes to people watch, who loves animal antics and who has the desire to read something filled with spirit and good humour. I recommend you set aside the day to binge on this brilliant book.'

Marie Carter, Editor, *Pets* magazine (www.petsmag.co.uk)

CHAPTER ONE

HOW HAD IT COME TO THIS?

"If we could talk to the animals, learn the languages. Maybe take an animal degree"

from Doctor Dolittle, Leslie Bricusse

"You know, there's not a hair left on his bottom now."

Our meal out seemed to be going well, as far as I could tell. My brother had suggested the Koh i Noor, one of Morpeth's top restaurants, and there I was a few days after Christmas with his young veterinary assistant, Margaret.

"And there's definitely scabs on his tummy."

John, the brother in question, being a decent boss, used to invite any young assistant to join his family for dinner on Christmas Day if they were on call and on their own over the festive period, and prevented by the work rota from travelling home. Which meant I got to say hello.

"We don't think there's any blood coming out of his you-know-what, but we think he might have tapeworms."

And what girl would not have fallen for me that year, standing (nearly, if I stretched) six feet tall, bearing a Masai spear and shield and much tanned from five weeks in Kenya? I had tried the odd chat-up line with one or two of the female assistants on previous visits, especially if I hadn't actually brought a girlfriend along with me. But this time it seemed to be working, perhaps because I meant it. In a "key words" search, one might have come up with "young, female" (and indeed "fit") before "veterinary" in Margaret's case. So - fingers crossed.

It was a bit disappointing that she didn't seem to know where Anfield was, but you can't have everything, and you wouldn't really want to go out with a girl who knew more about football than you did and wanted to argue about a referee's interpretation of "clear goal scoring opportunity". True, there was a middle-aged couple at the next table who kept looking at us whenever they spoke but they didn't come across as particularly scary or inbred. I was moderately confident that I'd avoided trapping balti sauce in my beard, I'd been consistently witty and charming all evening and was planning my next conversational gambit.

"Shall I bring a poo sample in for you to look at?"

No, I'm sure that wasn't what I was going to say. That came from the woman at the next table, who was now clearly looking in our direction.

I pressed on regardless. "The stuffed paratha's very filling, isn't it?" I ventured. "Would you like more rice?" Not witty, but safe. The evening's still young, and I'll do better when I've had a bit more to drink.

The woman's voice again, *"Lucky us bumping into you like this, wasn't it?"* And, with these words, apparently aimed in our direction, the couple from the adjoining table rose, put on their coats and departed.

"Someone you know?" I asked.

And so it begins.

I could have dated a teacher, or a landscape architect. Or an investment banker. Well, probably not one of those. But anyone other than a vet. Someone that didn't need to check with you at the dinner table whether they had animal waste in their hair. Someone whose social conversation relied less frequently on stomach-churning anecdotes.

How had it come to this? I blame my brother.

Exactly why the Ankers family's first pet was called Tess I'm not sure. Although both my parents were avid readers, I don't recall either of them being Thomas Hardy fans, and I have a feeling she was named for a well-nourished music hall entertainer of the time, Two Ton Tess from Tennessee. A broad-hipped, overweight blonde thing she was – we're on Golden Labradors now, keep up – and the family fell in love with her at first sight. My most vivid recollection at this distance is the keen desire I felt to convert her into a cuddly Davy Crockett hat. No doubt about it, Fess Parker was my hero and, at the age of six, the only way I could actually *be* Fess Parker was to get the hat. With pocket money running to something in brass with a picture of a thrift plant and "three" written on it, Tess was my most promising option. For some reason I was not allowed to implement this brilliant wheeze and readers of a nervous disposition will be relieved to note that fat-bottomed Tess lived on to a decent age, especially bearing in mind post-war food rationing and a tendency to make a nourishing hotpot from almost anything.

We set out on life's adventure in a small village called Melling outside Liverpool. Being at that age below hedge height, we grew up believing we lived in the heart of the Lancashire countryside. It was much later that we noticed Liverpool was barely a stone's throw away. (OK, supply your own tedious stereotyping gag here).

If you've heard of our village it'll either be because you live there, which doesn't count, or because you watch the Grand National. The horses race across the Melling Road on their way to glory – or occasionally to a fate somewhat less satisfactory. (It's a little early in the book to be specifying the range of possible unhappy outcomes. In a book about vets, I'm sure there'll be plenty of time for that kind of thing later on.)

Living close to the course, there was always someone around the village who claimed inside knowledge on the National and had it on the most reliable authority from a source close to the man who cleaned the windows of the mother of a stable boy that one particular mount had been prepared especially for the "big one" and was worth putting your entire life savings on. Or you could just stab a pin into the daily paper. But what I mainly remember about Aintree is the gate man telling my parents to push my older brother, John, and me underneath the turnstiles and just pay for one of us. Happy days. I think I can safely write that now as I expect the turnstile man is long gone, so they can't touch him.

My parents kept bantams in a run in the back garden, but I don't think that was a great success. When the foxes didn't get them they tended to drown their own chicks in the drinking water. But we lived next door to a farming family and I remember being treated to a close-up view of baby chicks being incubated under heat lamps.

The farmer's son was convinced he was a horse. Even at primary school age I thought it was odd that he would stand whinnying and stamping his hoof – sorry, foot – when you were trying to show him your best Brooke Bond cards. (I acquired all my general knowledge from these, which may be the reason I'm hazy about anything that happened after about 1960. Well, one of the reasons).

In one of his more anthropomorphic moments he told me that, if you were in a car that went at 60 mph, your head would fall off. There was no way this hypothesis could be tested as his family were the only ones with a car, but since then I have on occasion been known to throw caution to the winds and risk it. (My daughter says she can't recall such a display of derring-do on my part but they always say stuff like that to annoy you). As a footnote here, I'll point out that it wasn't that family but the local bobby who had the whole village round to watch the

Coronation on their nine-inch wonder screen with a big magnifying glass on a frame in front of it. The star turn looked very pretty, as I recall. She seems to have done well for herself.

I think John's tropical fish came quite early on. What's that thing about creating one's stripper name by combining the name of your first pet with your mother's maiden name? If the fish arrived before Tess the Labrador, I'm not sure what that would have meant in terms of my alias. Bubbles Richards? Angel Richards? Neon? Quite complicated, I should think, as they were all bought at the same time.

There was much excitement in the household when we set up the tank with gravel, plants and water and an almost unbearable delay before actual fish could be added – we liked to do things properly. Staying up late to watch guppies being born was one of the highlights of the year. (There wasn't much on telly in those days once you'd got bored with the film of the London to Brighton train journey condensed into four minutes and the loss of your horizontal hold. For comparative purposes, younger readers should think in terms of the excitement of downloading a new app.) On the other hand, staying up through the night, boiling pans of water above a coal fire to maintain the temperature of the tank during a not-infrequent power cut, was just rubbish.

Then there was the great Melling frog plague of 1954.

Big bro had scooped a whole load of spawn from a nearby pond and brought it home to place in an old bath that sat in the back garden. A combination of benign neglect and school homework meant that the subsequent tadpole mountain evolved unobserved into an amphibian plague of near biblical proportions which generated a good deal of interest around the village, and not a little finger-pointing.

Talking of making one's own entertainment, as one is obliged to do in memoirs of this nature, I will draw a veil over an unsatisfactory attempt (John again) to catch pigeons by placing a trail of breadcrumbs leading into an upturned cardboard box, supported along one edge by what in technical terms would be called a stick, in the misguided belief that any decent, co-operative bird might be expected to knock over the stick and thereby seal its own fate. I am content to remain hazy over what future was intended for our prey. Perhaps my brother was already starting to show dangerously veterinary tendencies at this early age and had in mind not so much a pet as a subject for dissection. Success, in any event, eluded us.

There was a prospect of even more fun, living as we did a few yards from the Liverpool Leeds Canal, in hurling the occasional rock into the water, hiding and shouting "help!" Sadly, I'm pretty sure that nobody *ever* fell for this but what larrikins we were! (I've been keen to use that word for a while but now I've done it, I can't imagine why.) It was not unknown for John, being a few years older than me, to climb onto a passing barge, egged on by a rather more "worldly" lad who lived nearby (think proto ASBO), in order to pass alongside the Grand National course for a free view when the race was in progress – if you've followed the National on TV or radio you will have heard mention of Canal Turn.

Then there was "the tip" opposite our house, a "brownfield site" as we might now call it. At the time it was attributed to wartime bombing. German, presumably – it was never made specific, though we Merseysiders never entirely ruled out the Mancunians. The tip provided the prospect of dens, a steeplechase course and our own football pitch. After a morning spent discussing team strip, an appropriately elaborate goal celebration and which league to enter, and ten minutes clearing away stones, we were called home for lunch and the moment passed.

Let's move on, to London.

I don't think I was unhappy to be relocated when Dad's job took him to the leafy southern idyll he was promised in Wandsworth, particularly because it meant the end of piano lessons at the hands of the lady next door, whose house smelled distinctly funny. When I raised this as a perfectly reasonable justification for not going to piano lessons any more, and joining my friends outside to play footy with the communal village tennis ball instead, Mum explained that the weird smell was furniture polish.

So, in 1957 the family found itself living in the south-western suburbs of London, in Teddington. (The house cost £2,500 but I bet it's worth more than that now. It's a pity they didn't hold on to it.) The only fixed points we had in terms of the move were Dad's job in Wandsworth and a school for John and me in Hammersmith. In what seemed, for my parents, a surprisingly cavalier approach, they spotted on a map an area to the south west with a lot of green on it, caught a bus outside the school and waited to see where it took them. So, Teddington it was, thanks to the number 27 bus.

I'm hoping at this point that the only interesting thing I can tell you about the 27 bus, that Matt Monro used to drive one, is in fact true. Sadly, I suspect that, like watching QI, I'll discover that everything I know for certain is in fact wrong. I'm not sure how I'll get by if it transpires that swans can't break your arm with their wings. Or that Posh wasn't miming.

My appealing Merseyside accent didn't long survive the move south, though I still recall with resentment being marked down in a public-speaking competition at school for what the adjudicator described as a misguided attempt at Liverpudlian. *Love Me Do* was, sadly, still five years in the future and I had lost my distinctive Merseyside timbre well before I might have become fashionable. (Fellow scouser Billy Fury hadn't managed to swing it for me, and definitely not Frankie Vaughan.) Indeed, my strongest Liverpool-centred recollection from that time was begging my mother, unsuccessfully, not to make me go into school on the Monday after the Reds had tumbled out of the FA Cup to terminally useless, non-league Worcester City. Ten-year-old schoolchildren can be very cruel.

We lived next door to the groundsman responsible for a major sports centre and playing fields facility which stretched from our garden wall down to the Thames close by Teddington Lock. Though formally banned by him from ever setting foot on his hallowed turf, a daily scramble over the wall offered unlimited access. It also meant that we happened one day on a straggly line of ducklings (aw!) which had presumably started off somewhere near the river but were now clearly devoid of both a mental compass and a visible mummy or daddy duck. While I would no doubt have happily settled down to pen a carefully crafted letter aimed at identifying those in a position of responsibility with a view, perhaps, to setting up a task force to develop a road map to deal with this challenge, big brother simply scooped up the squeaking tinies, took them back over the garden wall and found a bucket for them to float about in, on the reasonable assumption that this would replicate their natural habitat. Worryingly, after an hour or two, they seemed not to be thriving. Indeed they looked positively miserable. This was no problem for the budding vet. Out came Mum's hairdryer (I can safely say Mum's. Chaps just didn't in those days, believe me; you just lay in front of the coal fire and risked self-harm) and we effectively toasted them.

The next day or so is best forgotten. Let's just say that we eventually let the two survivors loose, back on the playing field where we'd first found them, and wished them well. I'd like to think there are now thousands of their ducky descendants prospering all over the south east with a strange fascination for electrical appliances. But I guess it's unlikely.

We were allowed to have stick insects as being "less of a tie" than the Labrador, though as we didn't seem to go anywhere very much, I wasn't sure what the problem was. In fact we usually went to relatives in Middlesbrough for our main holidays. I only later came to resent this, when I discovered that my classmates were going to more exotic locations like Cornwall or the Isle of Wight and returning to school with those glass shapes full of bands of coloured sand. At least one didn't tend to get too overwhelmed with grief if the occasional stick insect turned out not to be resting but long dead, or got Hoovered up from the carpet. And we did have the usual assortment of terrapins and lizards, one of which gave Uncle Len a turn when it peered out at him from under the radiator when he was on the toilet.

There was also George, the green parrot, who spent little time in his cage and would alarm visitors by suddenly landing on their heads, where he would establish a firm perch by deploying his not inconsiderable claws. As George was disposed to seek the highest possible perch at any opportunity, our family became adept at taking up a sudden crouching position when anybody else came within striking distance, which would encourage George to switch allegiance, and perch, to the new victim. This led to a kind of strange whirling and dipping dance around the lounge which, viewed from the pavement outside, may have discouraged visitors, or burglars for that matter.

I have already touched on the significant role played in my life by those heroes in red, the legends of Anfield Road, Liverpool Football Club. This, as fellow sufferers know well, is not something you determine on the basis of a careful assessment of history, style or prospects. It just happens, and then you're stuck with it. At least I can truthfully say that my addiction began, not after the Mighty Reds had conquered English and

European football (and incidentally complemented the lovable mopheads, the Fab Four, in making Liverpool the centre of all significant culture), but when we – note the "we" – were in lowly Division 2, as it then was. This love affair began when we still lived on Merseyside, though for reasons I'm reluctant to speculate on, John decided he would be an Evertonian. I can only assume this may have been influenced by the fact that Everton were playing in the top flight while the Reds were struggling in the division below. Later on he was to switch his allegiance in the right direction but, if he's reading this, I thought it only proper to remind him.

Anyway, being only seven, I hadn't actually been to a match before we moved south and the first time I watched them live was when Dad took me to see them play a second division game at Charlton Athletic's ground, the Valley – a venue with a capacity, seemingly, of around fifty or sixty thousand and an average home gate of perhaps ten (thousand, that is). Row upon row of empty fold-down wooden seats and terraces adorned with moss and bird poo. Anyway, we won four nil (away!) and that's all that matters. I suspect (you'll appreciate that I haven't written the rest of the book yet) we may revisit the football thing later. So, for those who dread that prospect, look away now...

My brother and I went to big school in west London. When I think about it, which isn't often, it seems strange now to realise I was commuting by rail each day for over an hour from the age of nine, sometimes on my own. My commuting distances have steadily shrunk since then so I can now type this by dint of a day return from the kitchen to the lounge, with a better prospect of getting a seat, though admittedly without the benefit of picking up an impulse Jubbly as I pass the shop on the corner by Ravenscourt Park tube station.

I'd say we both prospered at school and Mum expressed some disappointment, on hearing of other people's sons becoming prefects, that John had been denied similar recognition. (We were always a family with social aspirations, you understand.) It was years later that my brother let me into a small secret. He had indeed been appointed to the prefecture, and thus the right to hang out in the special prefects' room and confiscate stuff, but he had headed straight to the pub nearby at lunchtime (aged about 16, I should think) to celebrate with friends, all in school uniform, and was spotted. Result: he was stripped of his prefect's badge on the same day but achieved some sort of fame for brevity in office.

Meanwhile, having reached the sixth form and being thus able to shed all those other inconvenient curriculum subjects, John set out to meet his veterinary destiny by attacking dead frogs with a scalpel. I recall him carefully reconstructing a mouse's skeleton from bones which he found in an owl's dropping. How cool was that? I think I was busy committing the local Ordnance Survey map to memory at the time, as well as learning the Morse code from the Schoolboy's Pocket Book on my daily commute, and the nations of the world and their capital cities. I was particularly intrigued by the footnote to the list in my school atlas of the most populous cities of the Empire, which explained that places like Calcutta had "true" (that is, presumably, ex-pat) populations of only a few thousand as most residents were "native souls". And to this day I'm always disappointed if a map doesn't include a line labelled in the key as "Western Limit of Indigenous Rubber" on it somewhere. It would surely add a certain something, say, to Harry Beck's London Underground map.

John never looked back – great A level grades and five years at the Royal Veterinary College, London. While based at the field centre out in the Hertfordshire countryside and doing his nocturnal stint keeping an eye on horses in foal, he became a source of disturbing stories of men visiting the livestock for romantic purposes. There was very little to warn us of that on my Geography course. Or, if there was, I missed it.

Perhaps it was down to his growing engagement with the animal world that our parents felt it appropriate to ask John to take Tess the Golden Labrador to the local vet when it eventually came time to "do the necessary" and put her to sleep. Or perhaps they thought it would be good for his character development and an essential element of the growing-up process. Either way, he flunked it. He got as far as the door of the vet's surgery, turned round and brought her home again - which, if nothing else, may have given him an early feeling for what soon-to-be-bereaved pet owners experience.

During the veterinary course each student is required to "see practice", observing the job as performed by a real live vet on his daily round with the intention of putting a practical gloss on all the theory ingested at college. Apart from the veterinary and agricultural knowledge gained through this process, seeing practice also taught you the right, and wrong, way of dealing with clients and to recognise some of the pitfalls to look out for when dealing with the general public. University students "in John's day" were in the extremely fortunate position compared with today's crop of being in receipt of an actual maintenance grant, but the sum available to fund this period, seeing practice rather than being able to get paid work somewhere, was small. The logical thing was to find a kind relative, or girlfriend with an understanding family, with whom you might stay free of charge while claiming this additional allowance. An uncle who worked in the estate offices of ICI, the then giant chemicals company, at Wilton on Teesside was able to put John in touch with the vet who did the farm work on the company's estate and he stayed there whilst seeing practice.

John had been "walking out", as I understand people may once have said, with Shelagh, the cousin of a school friend (whom I suspect to this day of being responsible for the "drunk in charge of a prefect's badge" episode – yes, Mike, it's you I'm talking about). At the end of his course he headed to Northumberland to his girlfriend's home territory to seek his first proper veterinary post. Something about the place must have appealed as he's still there, forty-five years later.

This was also the time I built my own aviary. I've never been a handyman but I did actually more or less design it, then help my father with its construction. OK, he did the tricky bits, but

I held the nails. I was very pleased with it. Most of the space was outdoors in my parents' garden but with a couple of bricks removed from the wall of an outhouse, providing access into a decently-sized cage inside. This became home for a variety of tropical finches which bred successfully. If the weather was poor, I would encourage the birds to move indoors and fasten a wire "gate" across the opening to ensure they remained warm and dry inside. One did need to keep an eye out that the bright yellow, male weaver bird hadn't followed his natural calling and single-handedly (with his beak, actually) fastened the gate by weaving straw through it, thereby sealing all of the birds on one side or the other.

Our time at university overlapped by just one term, though at different universities, and this term coincided with Dad's job relocating him from London back to Merseyside. My parents bought a house in the suburbs of Birkenhead, on the other side of the Mersey from Liverpool, and Dad travelled to work on the famous ferry.

The actual move north, back to Merseyside, was notable mainly for us carrying my aviary – at least, the indoor cage part – on the roof of my parents' small family saloon with the birds inside, covered by plastic sheeting to protect them from the wind. Each time we braked, the windscreen was immediately showered with bird seed from above, requiring the urgent attention of the wiper blades.

I went to Oxford to do Geography. I nearly wrote "to read

Geography" there, but that sounds like when they introduce themselves on University Challenge. It might have been handy, while there, to have paired up with some well-heeled young lady intrigued by my elusive northern charm. Sadly they couldn't spot it (my wife says she's still looking) though I used up my grant (younger readers, ask your parents) treating rich people's daughters to the 37s 6d Berni Inn special with prawn cocktail, black forest gâteau and Mateus Rosé in a funny-shaped bottle. Cool people were supposed to convert these bottles after use into lamps, but I've never been cool.

It wasn't difficult to get short-term work during the holidays. In addition to the usual student default job on the Christmas post, where I worked alongside a woman who said she was the aunty of Emerson or Lake or Palmer – or it could have been one of the Hollies - I tended the verges for the Birkenhead Parks Department until I lost control of a heavy duty mower and surged across the pavement towards a queue of school children at a bus stop. The week's highlight always came on Friday when the foreman gathered us together on site to hand over our brown envelopes stuffed with notes and coins (well, as much stuffing as you can with £8). I appeared to be the only member of the gang bemused by the instruction on the envelope, "Always check contents before opening as mistakes cannot be rectified afterwards". Strikes me that if we still paid everybody in the same way, the world might be the better for it.

I also worked briefly at the local labour exchange, providing maternity cover for the switchboard operator (not a success, and it's made me wary of phones ever since) and general dogsbody, making tea and ferrying the post round the building. Each envelope or sheaf of papers had stapled to it a list of staff who were required to initial their name in turn to show they had seen it before it went back into a tray to be collected by yours truly on the next round and delivered later to the next on the list. This could take weeks. The cover sheet of one packet had been annotated with a comment alongside one middle manager's name: "You appear to have initialled this sheet in error. Kindly erase your initials and initial the erasure."

Once good thing: having learned how the system worked, once my brief fixed-term contract came to an end, I moved round to the other side of the counter and signed on as unemployed.

"Hi Steve. Let's just check your form. You've signed to confirm that you've been here and available for work throughout the week? Yes, that's fine. By the way, how was the Lake District?"

Of course, as with any student-owned pet, the aviary was invariably left in my parents' care during term time whenever I returned to Oxford's dreaming spires, Tackleys all day breakfast and Saturday evenings being further depressed by Leonard Cohen LPs when we had nowhere to go that involved girls.

I can remember drinking quite a lot of beer in the students' union between intense debates aimed at forcing the Yanks out of Vietnam, and discounting in my wisdom the local real ale in favour of Double Diamond (Lord, forgive me). I played the odd game of Aunt Sally in the pub car park and croquet and tennis in the University Parks, but was eventually banned from the river because three of the punts I'd hired for a geography society party came floating back down to Magdalen Bridge in bits. For the remainder of my time there, whenever I needed a punt, I had to ask a friend to sign for it, then I would take it over after it had been poled out of sight round the corner. My daughter tells me that this counts as a "First World problem" - one unlikely to draw sympathy from those with more fundamental issues of concern. She's right of course. I suppose it may also suggest that my devil-may-care hedonism in the Swinging Sixties didn't quite rival that of, say, the Stones, or the college bridge club.

I do however claim to have been awarded three virtual quarter-blues for tiddlywinks while at Oxford. And I predict that is the first time you will have seen that written down in any autobiographical work – well, any autobiographical work involving vets anyway. Let me take you back, if I may, to the sacred hallow (can that be singular?) of the school prefects' room. Unlike John I managed to remain a prefect for days, weeks even, at a time and the key – possibly only – attraction for me was the tiddlywinks table which occupied much of the space and most of our lunch hours.

Mock not. This is an ace activity, combining all the tactical nous of a very bad game of chess with the physical dexterity of, erm, well, something that needs a bit of dexterity anyway. Aficionados will not need me to elaborate, and I haven't the inclination to waste time on you others. Unfortunately, isolated as we were in our cloistered boys' own environment, we developed techniques for potting, squopping and particularly de-squopping that simply wouldn't pass muster in the wider world. When we moved on to our various places of higher education we found our trick shots frowned upon and were obliged swiftly to learn the proper rules or get out. Happily I chose the shining path to righteousness and soon earned my place in a highly competitive university team. I was almost certainly the only one who didn't possess his own squidger, such was the expected level of commitment, but I successfully held down my place on the team, playing home and away against other university sides. A blue is awarded in proper grown-up sports if you represent either Oxford or Cambridge against the other. I understand that a half-blue may be awarded in less "prestigious" or traditional sports (I'm trying to choose my words carefully here). As a consequence our winks (please note: not tiddlywinks – I used that word before merely for clarity of communication) team awarded itself quarter blues (in my case, three years so three quarter-blues), though I prefer not to investigate whether these are recognised by anybody else.

Chuff arrived at the parental home in the Wirral at this time – though he was always officially mine. Chuff was a Border Terrier – a red, rather than a blue, though not in the sense that normal non-dog-owning people would understand those terms. "Red" means brown, while "blue" means brown with some darker bits. Anyway, Chuff was simply weird. Or differently normal.

He was "sourced" by John – my big brother, the vet, if you recall – from a breeder he knew locally. Officially he was

Ulgham Red Wanderer, or something like that, after the village in Northumberland that he came from. His pedigree was way better than mine. I don't think Borders were seen as frequently around the country as they are now. I was a tad reluctant to accept a small dog but the family in-house vet described the breed as "canny".

He (Chuff, not John) had an extraordinary nose for the things that he most valued in life, namely rubber and, being largely ignorant of its toxic qualities, chocolate. All right, he may have inherited the latter from me, but definitely not the former. He could be guaranteed to home in on any cupboard in any house where either of these had once lain. And he didn't let go. Persuading him to give up, go home, think about something else for a while, was a waste of time.

Christmas morning was an entertainment. I would wrap something of interest to him – anything you like, provided it was made of rubber - in as many layers of paper as I could find and place it among the presents at the foot of the tree. Then, at an appropriate moment he would be told to go find, with resulting chaos. The things we did for fun in those days before we had YouTube.

In hindsight, and knowing that Chuff's mental acuity may have left him a Bonio short of a full packet, I suppose I shouldn't have put too much store by his ability to reflect and advise. At the time, however, and going through all the social trauma and girlfriend issues of an undergraduate (that's me, not him), I relied heavily on Chuff to hear me out and counsel me during my trips home from university. I do not recall him ever giving me poor advice.

After I had completed my geography degree, reluctant to embrace the world of proper work, I went on to University College London to do a two-year postgraduate course in Town Planning.

Readers may be familiar with the concept of the Freshers' Fair – or Fayre if you went to a naff university - where the new intake at a seat of higher education are confronted by an array of societies and organisations keen to enlist them. There's a bit in *Chariots of Fire* where Harold Abrahams signs up for Gilbert and Sullivan. I experienced my own Harold Abrahams moment, but without the singing, or the film crew following me about, so nothing like *Chariots of Fire* really. Anyway, I wandered through the plethora of bible enthusiasts, political groupings and people who thought maths would be more fun if you could do it in your spare time as well as in lectures, until I happened upon a - I know, get out more – tiddlywinks table and I casually squidged a few winks.

"Played before?" they asked.

"Uh uh" I replied, displaying all the benefits of a three-year Oxbridge education. I asked about the club and its prospects.

"We made the semi-final of the Prince Philip Silver Wink last year, we've got five of last year's first team staying up and we've got a bloke called Steve Ankers coming on from Oxford. Do you want to join?"

Well, say what you like – and I expect you may be doing –

but a chap could die happy after that. Anyway, I spent my two years at London University (not all the time, just when playing) as first pair with Dave Clutterbuck, and we were good! In 1971 the team reached the semi-final, again, of the Silver Wink, competed for between university sides, but, due to play Londonderry - away - in the semi, we opted not to travel (check out that date by Googling the words "troubles" and "Irish") so we'll never know whether we might have cracked the big one. But I do still possess, in the chaos that passes for my study, the University College London Blue Bowl won by yours truly in the annual college singles tournament in 1972 and, embarrassingly, never returned. Enough! Not another winks-related word. Ever. I promise. Not one.

My two years at UCL ended in my collecting my degree at a ceremony held in Albert Hall - yes, that Albert Hall - from the Queen Mother as Chancellor of London University. My parents had tickets and were thrilled to attend.

Throughout the whole lengthy procession of new graduates across the stage the diminutive royal personage remained seated, smiling and nodding gently at each in turn. However, when it came to us postgraduates, she clearly felt more was required of her, put on a pair of gloves and stood - at a higher level than the students, for obvious reasons - to shake hands. I reckon that of the hundred or more new postgrads that passed her way, she actually spoke to two. One was in a wheelchair, the other was me, probably because I was either at or near the beginning of the alphabet. The conversation went roughly along the following lines:

"Congratulations, and what are you doing now?" (That from the Queen Mother, not me. I guess the answer would have been fairly obvious the other way round).

Me: "Thank you. I've managed to get a job in a local authority planning department."

QM: "And did you find your degree useful?"

Me: (Bear with me, I know this isn't exactly Oscar Wilde): "Yes, it was a very practical, vocational course".

QM: "I'm so pleased."

It was another hour or so before the ceremony ended and I met up with my parents outside. I say "met". Actually my mother came hurtling towards me:

"Quick, before you forget, what did she say to you, what did you say, what did she say back ..."

To which it seemed only polite to reply, "She asked how you were, Mum. I told her your angina was still troubling you but that you sent your regards".

CHAPTER TWO

STARTING OUT

*"A few alligators are naturally of the vicious type and
inclined to resent it when you prod them with a stick.
You can find out which ones these are by prodding them."*

Will Cuppy, 1884 – 1949

"I always let off some gas before I perform a gastrotomy"

Veterinary surgical lecture, 1978

It was my first ever day at work, not counting student holiday
jobs, and I wasn't taking chances. I'd bought and studied the
relevant map and left myself plenty of time. A little apprehensive
about entering the world of real work, I set out good and early
from my rented room next door to the family planning clinic
on Palatine Road in Didsbury, south Manchester.

When I arrived at the railway station there didn't seem to be
much activity for a morning rush hour and, oddly, the station
building seemed to be disguised as a florist's. I peered over the
wall onto the platforms below. Somehow it didn't look right,

with the complete absence of rail track and the brambles spreading across the platforms, but it might explain the lack of hurrying commuters. B******s. Suddenly my time in hand didn't seem so generous. But Mancunians are a pretty approachable bunch and I was soon pointed towards the appropriate bus stop for the city centre. My arrival for work deteriorated into a sweaty, stressed-out run but I just about made it in time.

"I missed the train" I explained.

"By about three years" they said.

On finishing my university town planning course in London I had made the kind of decision that can have a major bearing on one's life. Should I look for employment in or near the capital where I had spent the past two years, or head into the unknown? It's hard in these days of high levels of graduate unemployment to believe that one actually had a choice of jobs back in the 1970s, in both private and public sectors. I felt instinctively that I was a public sector kind of chap, and basically still do – still equipped with my original seventies beard (I hear it's back in fashion at last?), though now tinged with the odd streak of grey tastefully applied, and subscription to *The Guardian*.

The geographical element in my make-up told me that there was somewhere handily located for the family home and football club on Merseyside, my brother's place in Northumberland and my recent base and university friends in London. That somewhere looked large enough to host big city attractions but, unlike London, was small enough to escape from if I needed to breathe the open country air. That place was Manchester, and it was splendidly located for hill walking in the Lakes, the Peak District, Snowdonia and the Yorkshire Dales. I had actually visited the city just once before, for an FA cup semi-final between Liverpool and Everton, and had been impressed, on heading from Piccadilly Station to the bus stop, to spot the offices of the Blood Transfusion Service located in Gore Street. True, I couldn't stand their most famous football team, but otherwise I loved my time in Manchester. I intended to stay for a couple of years before moving on; I stayed for twenty.

The first year or so of my working life was spent in an almost empty and seriously clapped-out Art Deco 1930s "skyscraper" called Sunlight House while in the pay of Lancashire County Council. I won't call it "working" for the County Council because I'm not sure I did any work. Local government was about to undergo a complete overhaul across the country and I was sitting in a moribund "divisional" (branch) office which was facing certain extinction only a year down the line. I'm sure the grown-ups in the office were busily engaged either in implementing this major reorganisation or organising their own imminent retirement, but I was much too junior to count.

I remember we had a well-used pub location map on the notice board for the purpose of site visits and we owned a shared office tie in case any visitors turned up. One of my colleagues displayed a huge calendar on his desk, on which he conscientiously ticked off the days to his retirement. He was in his early thirties.

Sunlight House itself was named, not after a bar of soap – don't be silly - but after the owner and architect, Joseph Sunlight, who was well into his eighties and occasionally spotted wandering the corridors with a small entourage, providing a pretty good model for Young Mister Grace in *Are You Being Served?* Joe's parents were Belarussian refugees from conscription by the Tsarist authorities. Conscientious research (Wikipedia) tells me that on arrival in the United Kingdom they may indeed have taken their name from Port Sunlight, the home of soap, but that's different. As their own surname was Schimschlavitch, this may not have been a bad move on their part. In a brief, one-year tenure as Liberal MP for Shrewsbury, Joe's main claim to fame appears to have been in introducing a Private Member's Bill on the standardisation of bricks.

"Joseph, that's great news about your election victory! Your mother and me, you won't believe how proud you've made us. And what a wonderful country this is – we came here only a few short years ago, fleeing for our lives, and now here's our son elected by the Great British people to represent them in the Mother of Parliaments."

"Thanks pa."

"Now, tell me son, what's the first thing you plan to do now you've become so famous and you're a Member of Parliament in our new homeland? How will you repay the kind people who trusted you to represent them; how will you help to make this fine nation a safer, happier place; how will you bring good to the world?"

"I was thinking of bringing in a bill to standardise brick sizes."

"OK..."

Sadly, the bill was lost when Joe was defeated in the 1924 general election. The world could have been such a different place, a better place. If only, Joe, if only ...

I still have a copy of the original 1930s Sunlight House prospectus for potential business tenants which sets great store by its running hot and cold water and its state of the art Otis elevators – lifts. These remained in place when I was there in the early seventies; splendid wood-panelled constructions with an impressive set of iron gates, still manually operated by a man with even more impressive, huge and hairy hands.

There was a disused and derelict swimming pool in the basement. We would dare each other to explore it by torchlight in true Famous Five manner when we returned from our usual lengthy Friday lunchtime session of fried egg and bacon butties washed down with several pints of one of the local real ales – sadly, a fine tradition now much honoured in its passing.

Disappointingly, my gentle introduction to the world of work didn't last. From the various scruffy fragments of north-eastern Cheshire and south-eastern Lancashire arose the shiny, new, thrusting Greater Manchester with its very own Greater Manchester Council and a set of ten more or less new Metropolitan District Councils to go with it.

GMC, as it styled itself in an echo of the longer established GLC in London, was nothing if not dynamic. I cut my professional teeth in a junior post in its environmental team working on an ambitious programme to convert more than a century's worth of industrial dereliction into a network of country parks and open spaces. Derelict land was reclaimed for public benefit, new paths were created, fine old buildings were restored and visitor facilities appeared. A million trees a year went through the County Council's own tree bank to be planted on reclamation sites. The scale of the programme has probably never been equalled in Britain.

I hadn't intended to stay in Manchester that long, but why would I ever want to leave a job like this?

The first Christmas of the new organisation was spent in temporary office accommodation above a cinema in the centre of Manchester, prior to locating the workforce to a new County Hall in Piccadilly Gardens. That Christmas was marked by a short but hilarious revue put together in a hurry by a few of the staff who had just joined the new body from the Town Hall, the home of Manchester City Council. There are no doubt similar panto-style productions in workplaces up and down the country, or at least there used to be. Mention the typing pool supervisor and you're guaranteed a laugh, especially if her name appears in the opening credits for the show alongside the words "Fights arranged by..." You get the picture.

I thought this was brilliant and the following November, with no previous history whatsoever, I asked the perpetrators if I might join them. I sat down and wrote a sketch based on the idea of a sad and lonely council employee (no relation, I can assure you) who became addicted to the planning system, who started sniffing development plans, smuggled planning applications home with him, just to be near them, and gave his girlfriend a listed building consent for her birthday. It was performed as a two-man dialogue with me as the sad git and a colleague using my desperate plight as the basis for an appeal to the audience for support – a hatstand perhaps, some red tape that you don't know what to do with – for the poor souls incarcerated in the Nicholas Ridley (think Eric Pickles) Home for Distressed Planners in Bridlington.

Things could only improve. I was welcomed to the fold and continued to write and perform for the office Christmas shows for many years, and I'd like to think we got better.

In fact we developed a bit of a name for our "art" and were soon invited to perform at the annual town planning summer school, a national gathering of practising planners held each year on a different university campus. From that we received invitations to entertain local branches of the planners' professional body. We came pretty cheap, as I recall – usually a bottle of something each – so perhaps it wasn't that great an honour. We performed in locations as exotic as Nottingham, Lancaster, Exeter, St. Andrews, Edinburgh and Cardiff as well as London. While jokes about office celebrities or bosses might work all right back in County Hall, where we were still performing at Christmastime, we had to "up our game" for these wider audiences and work up material relating to national bureaucrats and topical issues and sneering at government ministers.

The summer school shows were our favourites. When a group of fellow professionals had been incarcerated together for a week grumbling about the speakers, the accommodation or the catering, they were likely to be a receptive audience for our end-of-school show. It was a joy to perform in front of three or four hundred town planners all contentedly shouting "He's behind you!" as loud as they could, or spotting the president of your professional institute acting out a death scene in the front row in response to your "Planning in the aftermath of the nuclear holocaust" sketch.

And then there was the Great Lace Market Disaster. I have nothing against Nottingham's Lace Market; it's a fine theatre. It was our own fault.

We had been invited to perform for the regional branch of the planners' professional institute and this was their choice of venue. For some reason – illness, probably, or holidays, or some phobia about men in green tights – we knew our line-up was going to be diminished. We didn't have our usual musicians with us or any technical back-up (the bloke who did the lights). We hoped we could rely on the strength of the written material – the news items and sketches – and our own delivery.

However, we hadn't built in any way of telling the audience when it was time to laugh. So, the first brilliantly crafted news item, wittily performed. Silence. The second item. Again, some smiling faces, but silence. And, once an audience has started in this vein, it becomes well-nigh impossible to persuade them to let rip. We may have been rank amateurs but we could tell that this wasn't right. This same material performed elsewhere had brought loud, uninhibited laughter, which tended to improve the delivery of the next bit. Once any allegedly humorous line is received in silence, it prompts a desire to flee the stage in search of a dark place some distance away.

We learned from the experience. By the end of the evening we had begun to encourage the audience by starting the clapping ourselves from behind the stage. For future shows we twigged that even switching off a light can signal the end of a sketch and legitimise the process of chuckling.

Years later I found myself chatting to a friend and fellow planner who told me that he had been present that evening. He said they'd all enjoyed it. We hadn't.

For the purposes of our shows we exploited a not entirely fictitious place called Grotton.

Now, Grotton does exist. It's a humble little place located between Oldham and Ashton under Lyne, and one of our team knew the area from childhood cycling holidays, or something. The terms "grot and grotty" had some currency at the time so Grotton took on the useful role of providing a setting for our pokes at local government and the planning system. Rather than saying "Here's an amusing thing about planning", it became "and news today from the city of Grotton where Chief Planner T Break said ..."

So, in effect we created our own virtual conurbation, with a range of local authorities of different political persuasions. We peopled the various neighbourhoods with characters who would enable us to tell our tales and make the occasional witty but, hopefully, telling point. If we needed an architect, a NIMBY residents' group or a big bad developer, no problem; we just created one.

We were invited out to lunch at a smart restaurant in Manchester's Chinatown by a producer working for Granada TV to discuss a possible small screen appearance. As they were footing the bill, I thought I'd try something different and ordered some rice wine with my meal. An elegant Chinese-patterned teapot and small glass arrived. I waited a few moments, then poured and started to take cautious sips. I wasn't excited. I'd expected something with more bite than the bland taste I was getting, but pressed on nevertheless through lunch.

Towards the end of our meeting another member of our team called across the table.

"How're you finding that? To your taste?"

"Can't say I'm impressed. You'd have to shift a fair bit to have an impact."

"Can I try it?"

The pot was handed across the table. My colleague poured himself a shot and took a sip. After a while his brow furrowed and he lifted the lid of the pot.

"You might want to see this," he said, and passed the pot back without the lid.

Ah. Inside was an attractive little pod containing a tepid but quite potent quantity of rice wine. It would no doubt have been at a more appealing temperature had I not drunk most of the warm water which had been stopping it from going cold.

As our lunch was nearly over, I downed my newly-discovered tipple in a hurry and duly pronounced it an improvement. Few people can carry that sort of thing off with dignity. I'm not one of them.

We turned some of our ideas into a book one year, *The Grotton Papers*, but Mrs Thatcher chose that very year to "come out" as Prime Minister and did her best to steal our headlines. We never forgave her. Though that may have been for other reasons.

It was also the year I managed to wreck a knee playing mixed volleyball in a fun NALGO (then our local government trade union) sports competition, to match an identical injury to the other knee from a few years earlier, picked up in a rugby seven-a-side tournament at school. I must have a design fault. Or several, if my wife is to be believed. Anyway, months of enforced inactivity followed by surgery and a lengthy recovery process contributed to me becoming very unfit. (One of the great things about getting older is that now I don't have to come up with reasons.)

I was on the third or fourth round of beers with two friends in my local Holts pub, the Griffin in Heaton Mersey, where I made all my best decisions, when one of them began talking about his training for the New York marathon which was being covered by the regional television news programme. Armed with a significant intake of liquid confidence, and conscious of just how unfit I was, the decision came easily. "Right" I said, "that'll be me next year. In twelve months you can put me down for the – where was it again? The New York marathon thingy. Whose round is it?"

This is not the book for a detailed account of our build up to the big day. Even I wouldn't read that. Suffice it to say that we never did compete in New York. But we did, within six months, run – and I think that's a reasonable word to use as I didn't ever actually walk other than at the drinks stations – the Manchester (Piccadilly) marathon. Six months on and we went to Dublin and did that one, and another six months later we ran the Piccadilly again. I know you're not going to ask but, hey, it was hard work, so the answer is 3 hours 57 minutes, then 3 hours 29 minutes, then 3 hours 20. By which time I had worked out that going to the pub the night before running a marathon to help me relax tended to mean I started off hung over and already dehydrated, which isn't clever, and the constant pounding on the pavements of Greater Manchester was doing my knees no good at all. That's where Holt's bitter gets you.

There is a postscript. Recently I attended a weekend course in Brighton in Teaching English as a Foreign Language, a qualification which I felt might usefully facilitate the odd foreign trip. On the Saturday they asked us to bring something that could be used for a kind of "show and tell" teaching session on Sunday. I took a rather heroic photograph of me crossing the 1981 marathon finishing line in Dublin, in around 4,000th position, wearing a rather fetching sweatband around my forehead which, along with the abundant head of hair and luxuriant moustache which I then sported, contributed to an overall image of rugged athleticism. Come my turn, I held up my object of pride. With one voice the other students shouted out "One one eight, one one eight!" I was mortified. But I could see their point.

We left my brother in Northumberland starting his first proper vet job, working and living in Morpeth and marrying Shelagh from Whitley Bay. They soon started a family – by acquiring Satan, who laid claim to being mostly a Black Labrador, and who was in truth, something of a hypochondriac. If he looked a bit sorry for himself of a morning, Shelagh would send him to see John, who would pretend to examine him, pat him on the head and send him on his way with a sugar lump or some other placebo. Job done.

Satan was soon followed by other Black Labrador lookalikes in Cerberus and Lucifer. See what they had going on there?

They also had a parrot named Sam, a replacement for George the scary head hopper from Chapter 1. Sam had a penchant for lowering his head upside down into the household's various tropical fish tanks so he could trawl them, which is a nice trick if you can pull it off, though clearly unsustainable in terms of maintaining fish stocks.

Being a single chap working in Manchester, it was fairly easy for me to travel up to Morpeth for the weekend and I would occasionally accompany John to the surgery or go out with him on a call. In those far off, pre-mobile phone days it was hard to go far from home if you were "on call". Being a vet usually involves not only working pre-arranged surgery hours, visiting farms or seeing clients and their animals with appointments, but being available for out-of-hours emergencies. This cover would be provided on a rota basis and if it was your turn you were required to be close to a phone so you could be contacted. The best you could manage, by way of securing some freedom of movement in the days before pagers and cell phones, was to have a loud bell fitted to your house phone so you could at least be in your own garden ready to dash in if it rang, or you could provide your colleague or answering service with the phone numbers of the people you were going to spend the evening with or the restaurant you would be dining at. Ah, those were the days.

Although, as a student in the 1960s, John had grown his locks reasonably long and could fill a tie-and-dye T-shirt with the best of them, client perspective demanded that he turn up at farms with hair more like a 1950s footballer and dressed in a sports jacket with elbow patches if he was to be trusted to be let loose on their precious livestock. I confess at this point that my pinko Guardian-reading political and environmental tendencies didn't always sit naturally with the social conversation of the Northumbrian farming community, but they were very good about it.

I discovered one of a vet's box of "magic tricks". Having diagnosed milk fever – in a dairy herd, surprisingly enough – when a recently-calved cow is subject to sudden collapse brought on by a drop in calcium in the bloodstream, the vet administers the appropriate injection and can watch with some confidence as the comatose cow, close to death, will start to show twitching of the muscles, beading of sweat on the nostrils, followed by a belch of rumenal gas, defecation, and a struggle to a sitting position – much as you will see on any Friday evening in the middle of Newcastle. The patient will then rise to her feet and walk away, all in five to ten minutes from a horizontal start. I've watched Christopher Timothy do it on TV in *All Creatures Great and Small* and my brother could do it just as well.

I learned that the sheep is the only commonly-domesticated commercial animal that is a seasonal breeder – that is, it gives birth at a set season of the year, namely between February and May. (Don't say this book isn't educational.) John would describe lambing as one of the most satisfying parts of the job - sorting out a jumble of legs and heads belonging to twins or triplets and delivering healthy lambs one at a time. A lambing that consists of trying to ease a large lamb out of a narrow pelvis, by inserting a hand and manoeuvring a head or bringing a foot through the birth canal, may be equally satisfactory but can be very painful on both the hand and the ewe!

Nowadays, with the average flock size greatly increased, shepherds are much more experienced, which means that the only time the vet is called to assist is likely to be when things are really tight and it appears that a caesarean is going to be necessary. Later, as we will see, John acquired his own flock of pedigree sheep – possibly because he would then be able to experience some nice easy lambings and not be left with just the complicated ones that the shepherd didn't fancy. Also, having his own flock made him realise that in some ways the vet gets the easy job – once he departs, the shepherd's or farmer's real work of persuading ewes to adopt orphan lambs and keeping the lambs alive and healthy can begin.

Another side-effect of working with sheep every day, John would maintain, is that one comes to appreciate them for what they are and not just the stupid animal with an inclination towards self-destruction that many believe; that they are truly a pleasure and a privilege to work with. Research shows, apparently, that sheep come higher up the scale in memory and cognitive ability than other domestic animals like the horse, cow or chicken – which must come in handy if they've mislaid their glasses or need to find their own way to the shops.

STOP PRESS

I had just written that previous paragraph when John called me back to tell me that was all rubbish.

"I've just come in from the lambing shed," he muttered down the phone. "I've spent half an hour trying to persuade an old ewe that the five lambs she has corralled in a corner are not all hers as she hasn't even lambed yet, and tell a mad gimmer that her own lambs are there to be nurtured and are not demons from hell to be avoided at all costs. I've changed my mind. Sheep are totally stupid and it's a wonder they're not extinct... at least, that's my thought for today, and will be until lambing is over and I get to see a gang of healthy lambs chasing each other round the field on a warm May evening, when suddenly they will be marvellous animals once again!"

The status of pigs in the average vet's life has also changed over the years. Nowadays, with large pig-breeding and rearing concerns, it's primarily a matter of preventative medicine, performance figures, conversion statistics and so on, and little hands-on work is involved – other than the blood testing of, say, fifty reluctant sows who let the vet know in no uncertain and deafening terms just what they think of the whole business.

But in John's early days as a vet, many of the allotments in the old mining villages like Ashington and Bedlington had sheds containing two or three breeding sows and their litters which would be reared for sale at the local marts. The vet would routinely be called upon to castrate the male piglets of such litters. Sows, it has to be said, are generally ill-disposed towards people who interfere with their offspring so, when about to castrate a litter, it was essential to get the sow out of the pen and make sure the door was firmly shut. With one particularly unfriendly sow, it was agreed with the owner that it would be prudent to ensure she was not only out of the pen but out of the building as well, so she wouldn't be excited by the noise of squealing piglets. This having been accomplished, with difficulty, they proceeded to the job in hand, the owner catching and holding the piglets while John did the necessary. As soon as the first squeal emanated from the first patient there was an almighty roar and a crash and both vet and owner found themselves face down in the pen. The sow had charged the corrugated tin wall of the shed at speed, causing it to collapse inwards, hitting them both on the way down and coming to rest propped up by the sty wall. From his prone position under the tin sheeting the vet had an inspiring view, three feet above, of an angry sow looking for whoever had upset her babies. Having wisely released the piglet, so causing the squealing to stop, the guilty pair were able to reach the safety of the door by means of an undignified retreat on all fours.

The other routine pig-related work in those early days was to attend the farrowing sow. Somehow this always seemed to happen at night. Finding a house number in the dark can be tricky, but finding the right allotment is something else altogether. "Go in from the east, take the second right, then third left, it's the green gate on the right and I'll be waving a torch". And those allotment "roadways" are narrow. Even if your veterinary expertise did not improve rapidly, you soon became pretty good at reversing.

On the down side, a vet gets to see some extraordinary cases of human behaviour not matching up to that of the animal kingdom.

Scene: On the operating table a small, bedraggled terrier, sedated and in great pain, was about to be anaesthetised so the vet could pin his shattered leg, caused by his owner throwing him from an upstairs window in a fit of rage. After what he had gone through, he had every reason to hate and mistrust all humans, but even in his sorry state, he was still wagging his tail and licking the nurse's hand as she gave him the anaesthetic injection prior to his operation. Luckily the vet was able to pin the leg successfully and his friendly nature meant he was adopted by the family of one of the practice nurses. He went on to live the full and happy life he deserved in the midst of a loving family.

"Lugless Douglas" was a five-year-old male Greyhound; a real gentle giant. He was brought to the surgery by the local dog warden, having been found on the streets of Ashington with two torn and bleeding wounds on the side of his head where his ears should have been. Obviously Douglas' racing days must have been over and, rather than re-home him or even take him to the vet to be painlessly put to sleep, the owner decided to abandon him. However, since registered Greyhounds can be traced by tattooed numbers in both ears, the owner had hit on the ingenious idea of hacking off his ears to avoid him being traced back.

One day a hiker arrived at the surgery, reporting that he had come across an elderly Golden Labrador tied to a tree and in a very sorry state. Following his directions John had searched the local moor for quite some time until the sound of a dog whining led him to the spot. He found the dog very cold and wet, shivering and extremely distressed. He untied her and took her home, placing a heat lamp over her and offering her food and water. Sadly the dog turned out to have a large ulcerated mammary tumour which was clearly malignant and inoperable so there was no happy ending, but one would still wonder how a pet "lover", rather than taking the animal to the vet to painlessly end her days, would reward a lifetime of love and devotion by taking her to an isolated wood to endure a slow and agonising death by exposure, dehydration and starvation.

On a more cheerful note, a good number of abandoned, mistreated or injured pets are adopted by vets, veterinary nurses and receptionists and, of course, are well placed to receive professional attention. Of John's own current canine "herd", Maisie is a lurcher abandoned after a road accident, Norman was brought to the surgery with a fractured leg by an owner who wanted him put down as "he'll be useless and it'll be cheaper to just get another one", and Stanley was abandoned in a churchyard with the rest of his litter when a day old.

It is of course vital to set a good impression as a young tyro in any business and I guess John must have passed the test somewhere along the line. As he has established himself in the Morpeth practice over the years, he has of course seen many "apprentices" arrive - and not all have flourished in that environment.

In the early days every member of the practice was expected to turn his hand to whatever arose and be able to treat cats, dogs, farm stock and horses with equal willingness and ability. This meant they were ideally looking, not for someone with a specialist qualification, but an all-rounder who could cope with the range and variety of veterinary general practice. One new arrival (let's call him Andy) stood out from other applicants, with his CV showing he had been qualified for three years and gained a PhD in physiology and was thus entitled to call himself Doctor. His arrival was eagerly anticipated with the expectation that he would bring something new to the business.

Andy's first task was to vaccinate a bunch of young calves against brucellosis. It was a simple job but, to identify vaccinated animals, once injected they had a special metal MAFF (Ministry of Agriculture, Fisheries and Food) tag inserted into the left ear. Since brucellosis was a nasty disease that could also infect humans, it was important not to scratch or inject yourself with the needle. Knowing this, Andy took the precaution of wearing a thick pair of gloves throughout the procedure and began to inject the calves and tag them while the farmer held them. Unfortunately, when tagging the fifth or sixth calf, he inadvertently stuck the tag through the tip of the finger of his glove, firmly stapling it to the calf's ear. The calf, unhappy at having a large object flapping around by the corner of his eye, gave a loud bellow and set off across the field like a cat with a tin can tied to its tail. It took the calf a while to slow down and even longer to catch. The farmer was unimpressed.

Another early job for Andy was de-budding young calves to avoid them injuring each other – anaesthetising the horn buds, then cauterising the tiny horn with a de-budding iron heated by a Calor gas burner. Half way through, as Andy stepped back from applying the anaesthetic to one calf's horn, he knocked against the iron which was heating up on its stand on the gas burner. This duly disappeared down his leg between over-trousers and welly and the farmer was startled to see the young vet give a loud yell and jump, with great presence of mind, into a handily placed cattle trough full of water.

After recovering from the trauma of this episode, he was next required to perform a simple herd blood test of a mere dozen cattle. The senior partner reasoned that anyone who had spent three years of his doctorate blood-testing awkward little animals like rabbits could draw blood from the large veins of a cow. Andy set off for the farm at 9 am, so it was disturbing to receive a call from an impatient farmer at 3 pm asking if someone could go and finish the job as Andy had managed only five or six cows all day.

A chastened Andy arrived back at the surgery to be told by the irate senior partner that, "being useless at anything else", he could at least go and remove the dew claws from a litter of pups in a nearby town. Relieved to have escaped fairly lightly, Andy set off, while the partner gradually simmered down. The door then re-opened, Andy's head poked round and he quietly enquired, "Which are the dew claws again?"

It was around this time that both he and the practice decided he wasn't cut out for general practice. He stayed for six months under supervision in order to qualify for MAFF, for whom he went on to work, rapidly rising to a senior position from which he now sends out instructions and guidance to the lesser mortals working out in the field.

In addition to farm animals, horses and the usual run of domestic pets, vets get to see a range of more unusual, exotic creatures and are expected to solve their problems.

Gandalf was a Griffon vulture, not generally viewed as the most attractive of birds with its naked head and scrawny neck and eating habits that might not pass muster at the Savoy. They can look majestic soaring high above but, seen at a carcase with crop bulging with meat and head stained with blood and gore, they are not everybody's idea of a much-loved pet. But vultures and other birds of prey are increasingly popular at public displays and, like any other bird, they can become unwell.

Although the popular perception is that vultures can happily digest aged and rotting meat well past its best-before date, they can pick up serious infection as the meat deteriorates and John treated Gandalf over a period of several days until he was able to make a full return to health. The sight of a recovering vulture scuttling round the recovery room begging the nurses for food was a memorable one.

Rocky the python was brought to the surgery in a large dustbin carried by three bulky, T-shirted and heavily tattooed men. He had a swelling on the side of his upper jaw. The initial examination took place with two of the men lifting his head out of the bin and holding on tightly for John to insert a gag in his mouth while the rest of Rocky remained in situ, rocking the bin alarmingly. It was decided that an operation would be required under anaesthetic. For this, the vet needed to know Rocky's weight. Dustbin and snake were thus placed on the scales and then, with the help of two strong veterinary nurses, the three men lifted Rocky from his prison and held him straight to prevent him coiling around anyone whilst the bin was weighed empty. He topped the scales at a mighty 57 kg and was three metres in length.

For the operation itself an additional table had to be brought in alongside the normal operating table so his head and all important lung area were fully supported whilst the rest of Rocky remained in the bin. It took three vets and three nurses to hold him while he was injected and an experienced exotics nurse – as distinct from an exotic nurse – was present throughout the operation to oversee Rocky's breathing. He recovered well from his surgery and is still growing and lunching contentedly on his diet of rats and rabbits (I never promised this would all be cuddly).

Having developed something of a reputation for dealing with various exotic creatures, including lizards and other reptiles, it should have been no surprise when John was approached by a film production company which was making a TV series about a wildlife police officer set in the north-east of England. Health and safety and animal welfare regulations required a vet to be on the set whenever animals were being used.

The opening episode involved the officer investigating reports of an alligator in a flat in Newcastle. Having agreed an hourly rate for his attendance, John looked forward to a quiet day observing alligators from a safe distance and consorting with the stars.

He turned up as arranged at 7 am at the studio, which was set in a warehouse on the banks of the Tyne. Wandering round the strangely deserted set, he eventually found a technician rushing round with a worried expression on his face. "Thank God you're here", he shouted, "the alligator's escaped!" The gator's handler had apparently had far too much to drink the previous evening and was simply out of commission.

They hurried along a corridor to a room where, on entering, they were faced with a nine-foot alligator half out of its travelling crate, which was shaped like a coffin. John ran to the back of the crate (do they teach you this at vet school?), prised open the lid and, grabbing the alligator by its tail, hauled it back into the crate and slammed the lid down. They then sat firmly on the top of the crate until help arrived – perhaps one of those few instances when putting on a bit of extra weight can come in handy.

Having skinned her nose forcing her way out of the crate, and with the vet's usual antibiotic wound spray being an untelegenic bright purple, the alligator then required treatment from John in the form of the application of six bottles of "Newskin" from the nearest branch of Boots. That's one of those errands I just wish I'd been sent on. "Excuse me, do you have anything for..."

Being now "on the books" as it were, John was next called upon to attend the filming of episodes of a TV series called *Distant Shores* which involved a London surgeon, played by Peter Davison (previously a stalwart of *All Creatures Great and Small*), and his family relocating to an island off the Northumbrian coast which appeared to be inhabited by stereotypical country yokels. The surgeon's wife, played by TV and film actress Samantha Bond was to be seduced into a lingering kiss with a local whilst performing a rectal examination on a cow, the way you do – which is where John came in. Not for the kiss, which is probably a good thing, but to help and advise with the examination.

A local farmer had provided several quiet, photogenic Longhorn cows for the scene and all was set. There was a break of several minutes whilst the star prepared herself with a stiff drink and a cigarette for the traumatic encounter. John provided a protective calving gown and found an arm-length rectal examination glove for her to wear, then stood back, out of shot, to observe proceedings.

Surprising as it may sound, inserting your arm up a cow's backside does not come naturally to everyone and the actress struggled with the task. The only way to ascertain that her arm was inserted in the right way, and with the correct degree of gentle force, was for John to take her hand in his (gloveless) one, gently insert it and then withdraw.

The scene was then completed in one "take" and the star was greeted by rapturous applause and a fresh cigarette for her bravery, whilst John stood ignored in the corner of the shed scraping smelly green stuff from his arms and hands. To this day, whenever Samantha appears on TV or screen, the family delight in proclaiming "John once held hands with her – up a cow's a★★★".

When the programme eventually ran on telly we all had to watch, of course. It was explained to us that John would be performing in one particular scene which involved transporting a calf from the island to the mainland in a small rowing boat. This would be an important scene and John's performance would be crucial. On our next visit north he would be prepared to sign autographs.

We watched, we waited, we saw the rowing boat, we observed the calf, which seemed to carry off its role with due aplomb. John had been totally successful in not hogging the limelight. What a pro. For all the usual animal welfare and handling reasons, John had been asked to accompany and control the young bovine star in the making, lying uncomfortably and unseen in the bottom of the boat. "Best supporting cattle prod" anyone?

All this can of course make the work of a vet look entertaining, even if sometimes hazardous. There are occasions however when it is extremely dangerous. Etorphine is a drug used legally only by vets to immobilise animals, inducing a state of catatonia. Described as many thousands of times more powerful than morphine, it takes about 5mg to down something the size of a rhino. It's fatal to humans, including vets, and it is essential when using it to know just how to react should an accident occur. John managed one day in the surgery to prick himself on a needle previously primed with Etorphine which had been disposed of in the nearly full "sharps" container. Immediately he could feel it taking effect and, with nobody else in the vicinity, could already tell he was losing consciousness. Professional training kicked in. He located the known antidote, filled a syringe and injected himself. It worked, or this book would read very differently.

Single (though, I insist, not on the shelf) into my thirties, I always spent Christmas at my brother's place in Northumberland, getting used to the annual disruption to Christmas dinner by emergency call-outs. He was an early developer, and now had two kids and a wife who didn't think Christmas was Christmas unless there were at least a dozen people sitting around the table. Our parents, who got stressed out if we had visitors (my father tended to shout "Who the devil's that?" if the phone rang), were more than happy to cede the festive hosting rights to John and Shelagh and I was very content to play the role of jolly uncle, bringing my own barrel of draught beer and carload of presents and sporting the occasional flashing bow tie at the dinner table.

It seemed consistent with my role to encourage my young niece and nephew to eat some of their mother's excellent Christmas pudding by telling them that sixpence pieces were invariably to be found therein. Search their portions as they might, they never seemed to get close, while I, against all odds, found coin after coin in my own helping. Shelagh's eyebrows lifted slightly, as she couldn't recall having put any in there. But that's just the kind of zany guy I was. (You had to be there).

But my years of bachelor freedom were about to be seriously challenged.

CHAPTER THREE

SHETLAND: WHERE EVEN IS THAT?

"All his life he tried to be a good person. Many times, however, he failed. For after all, he was only human. He wasn't a dog."

Charles M Schulz, 1922 – 2000

"Don't give bulls testosterone – all you do is give them wet dreams and a bad temper"

Veterinary medicine lecture, 1980

During the Northumberland Christmas that followed my Kenyan holiday, our meal at the Koh i Noor in Morpeth notwithstanding, Margaret and I had got on well. We didn't shout about it, but we made arrangements for her to visit me in Manchester a few weeks later on one of her non-working weekends.

These plans, sadly, were to be turned upside down when my sister-in-law Shelagh's father died in January and his funeral was scheduled for my planned weekend of romance. Knowing

Shelagh's family well, I had no thoughts of not attending, along with my parents, so Margaret and I cancelled her visit to Manchester and I headed back to the north east.

This turned out to be a memorable occasion. John asked if I would mind helping young Margaret ("You remember my assistant, Margaret, from Christmas?") with some of the laying out of the catering and he apologised to me for the inconvenience of having to hang out with her.

The undertaker arrived at Shelagh's parents' house in Whitley Bay where we were all gathered and asked for the burial certificate. After a lively discussion it was agreed that this vital piece of paper was not in fact to hand but undoubtedly resting quietly on the mantelpiece at John and Shelagh's house in Morpeth. On being pressed over the degree of importance to be attached to this document, the undertaker responded, "Well, he won't be getting buried today without it".

It was decided that John would drive immediately to Morpeth to collect the certificate while the rest of us would head for the chapel and crematorium in Whitley Bay in the hope that he would return with the paperwork by the end of the service, in time for the interment. I offered to do the Morpeth trip instead of my brother as I didn't regard myself as playing a leading public role in the day's events. This offer was turned down on the basis that I wouldn't know where to find the certificate and would have to deal with the alarm system and so on. Instead, I was promoted into lead family car, replacing John.

En route, following the hearse, the immediate family were

understandably distressed by this turmoil. I tried to strike a positive note by suggesting, "You know, knowing your father as I do, I rather think he would have been amused by all this – on a my-family-couldn't-even-bury-me-properly basis". In a way this had the desired effect because everyone seemed to agree this was probably true, but the release of tension brought guffaws, which developed rapidly into hysteria, and at the entrance to the crematorium the gathering of grieving friends, neighbours and other relatives looked up to see a carload of fellow-mourners approaching, all clearly roaring with laughter.

Those of us in the know were inclined during the service to glance towards the door in the hope of sighting John with the vital document and were wishing that the eulogies and songs might be dragged out a little. When proceedings eventually came to an end, and there was still no sight of John, the minister announced that "due to a technical matter" it would in fact not be possible to bury Mr T this afternoon but that the family wished to invite everybody back to the house anyway. We all then exited the chapel amongst much tutting and wondering about just what kind of technical matter might have arisen to prevent burial. From one younger relative I heard, "Are they not sure he's dead?"

Outside, the driver of the hearse was instructed to head off towards the far side of the grounds to await further instructions while a degree of chaos quietly reigned. Cars manoeuvred to form a convoy amid mutterings about things being 'done properly in my day'. However, at this moment, John arrived in a screech of tyres, brandishing the important piece of paper through the car window like a motorised Neville Chamberlain and exclaiming "Wait, come back! We can bury him now!"

I set out on foot after the disappearing hearse. It felt, despite all that had passed, wrong to break into a run, so I walked as briskly as seemed commensurate with retaining a degree of dignity. Unfortunately my speed seemed only to match that of the hearse. Had I been competing in an Olympic walking race I would undoubtedly have been disqualified for "lifting", but I still wasn't gaining. My mother, watching entranced from their car, said later that she struggled not to laugh.

The deed was eventually done and we were able to retire to the bleak, black humour of a decent wake. My brother claimed to have completed the thirty-five mile round trip from Whitley Bay to Morpeth in just over half an hour, including the house stop and being halted by the local police with a "So, who do we think we are then, Stirling Moss? Funeral, eh? Well, careful now sir, we don't want another one, do we?" I'm not sure they'd do that if it happened now.

The next few months meant a fair bit of to-ing and fro-ing for me between Manchester and Morpeth. I would occasionally drive up after work to do my courting and found it hard to resist a girl who always made a point of washing her hands after she'd been squeezing a dog's anal glands. Normally, I suppose, one only gets to see one's new "squeeze" after an hour or more spent in front of a mirror. But that's enough about my preparations: Margaret is just the same. To be fair, she did scrub up well between work and restaurant and would usually check with me between courses that she didn't still have poo in her ears.

On my visits to Northumberland I joined Margaret on the occasional farm visit, as indeed I had done over the years with John. If the "patient" was unruly and the muck was flying, one got to hear some interesting technical language from the vet. Her most embarrassing experience with my brother's practice would have to be the occasion when she was called out to a farm to carry out a caesarian on a cow that was struggling to give birth unaided. She eased the uterus outside the body in order to make the necessary incision but had omitted to hobble the beast, which at this crucial point decided to contribute to the birthing process by rising to its feet and setting off for a wander round the stall – with the farmer hanging onto its halter and Margaret carrying the not inconsiderable weight of the calf-containing uterus. Somehow they managed to put a call through to John, who sped through the lanes to supply an additional pair of hands.

A more satisfying memory is of another partner in the practice offering unsolicited help in the surgery on a dog which Margaret was examining. It had been brought in after being fed lamb bones, was in clear discomfort and was straining continuously. The partner, calling on his many years of experience in such circumstances, went straight to the nub of the issue, and the solution. "There's your problem" he said, inserting his little finger into the dog's anus and deftly hooking out a bone jammed sideways across its rear passage, thus releasing in an instant the build-up of faeces from the previous fortnight

– all held of course under the greatest pressure. There was a shout of "Hit the floor" and everyone other than the partner in pole position ducked. He may have been one of the bosses but, when your colleague receives the full package in the face and down his clothes, well, I think you're entitled to laugh. You don't have a choice, really.

I'd grown up with animals around the house of course and the world of vets was a fairly familiar one. While at Edinburgh University Margaret had "seen practice" in one or two places around the country and in California, and had worked in Shetland before coming to work for my brother. In the early days of our relationship – that honeymoon period before communication is reduced to texting "where r u?" and "rmembr milk" – I genuinely wanted to hear more about her time in Shetland.

"The thing with Shetland was the wind" she said. "I don't think it ever actually stopped. Even when the wind wasn't actually blowing, it was still, you know, really windy. For the first month I looked like I had chickenpox. It was a kind of wind rush effect on my face."

"So, do they have, like, seventy-three different words for wind? Like the Inuit? Except that's snow?"

"I'm just saying. There are no trees but those they do have are just bent right over because of the wind. It gets really windy."

I nodded sympathetically. Wind in your face, I thought. Must have been hell. How would Ernest Shackleton have coped if he'd ever managed to drag his sledge away from the soft south and make it this far up?

"Are you taking this seriously?" she asked.

"That's what you remember about your time there?" I pressed.

"No. What I mainly remember is how amazingly friendly everyone was. I'd be lambing on farms and crofts during the day and then, when I got back to Scalloway in the evening, there'd be a line of trailers parked outside my house with even more ewes waiting to be lambed. But next day I'd find stuff left by the front door for me – a few fish, or a sack of potatoes or a pile of peat for the fire. That was really nice of them, especially when you're fresh out of university, and a long way from home."

"Were you homesick?"

"At first. But clients were always giving me tea and cakes and a full spread at the end of each farm visit. Very nice, but it made the day very long. And it didn't do much for my waistline. I was lambing a ewe for the local doctor and afterwards we were having tea in his house. Somewhere in the conversation I mentioned that I'd missed my Rubella vaccine at school. He disappeared into his office, came back with a syringe and stuck the vaccine in my arm while I was eating my Tunnocks tea cake. That was a bit unusual. And I had a puncture late one night in the middle of nowhere on my way home from visiting a sick ewe up near the big oil terminal at Sullom Voe. There was only the one veterinary practice in the whole of Shetland at the time so you had to cover everywhere, including going out to the smaller islands on a ferry..."

"Hey, that must have done wonders for business in the local pharmacies, from what I know of your affinity for sea-based travel."

"Thank you for that. Anyway, the roads were brilliant because of the oil money, and they were empty. I hadn't been working there long before the boss set off for a short holiday. Somewhere hot, I forget where…"

"To get away from all that wind, I expect."

"…and I realised I was the only vet in Shetland. The next nearest would be on the mainland, or Norway. Orkney probably. That focuses the mind."

"Sorry, I interrupted. You had a puncture?"

"There was no jack in the van and it was absolutely pouring down. I set off walking with the dog towards a light in the distance. When I knocked on the door and asked for help, even in the dark the crofter seemed to know who I was straight away. As the island vet you get to be a bit of a celebrity, like the doctor or the dentist, especially if you're a woman. He called his son to help the 'wife vet' as I was known. They drove me back to my car, changed the wheel, then disappeared. Hardly a word spoken the whole time."

"Try knocking on a strange door in Manchester like that late at night. The curtains would be twitching and Neighbourhood Watch would be right on your case. Was there much of a social life?"

"It was a bit quiet at times once you'd finished working for the day, but after I'd been there a while I was invited to a party, so that gave me the chance to meet people…"

"I know what vets' parties are like!"

"…so I put on my posh frock and got ready to impress. When I arrived at this particular Saturday night 'thrash', the room was set out with chairs round the outside and each with a bible on it. Everyone was asked in turn to choose a favourite passage to read out loud before we settled down for more serious study. Being a devout atheist, when it was my go, I said I would find it more culturally rewarding to hear local people's choices rather than me simply trotting out my boring old favourites. But there was plenty of life in Shetland if you knew where to look for it and loads of local musicians, especially fiddlers, so it's not really a quiet place. And they have this amazing Viking fire festival every January in Lerwick called Up Helly Aa when very butch men dress up as Vikings and march through the streets with blazing torches. They tow a replica longship which they burn in the loch. There's no women allowed in the procession, but behind the Vikings basically anything goes in terms of costume. Locally it's known as Transvestite Tuesday apparently. They have similar Ups, or it might be Aas, in other places round the islands."

"I imagine, as an unattached, young woman who scrubs up quite well, if I may say so, you would have been making a welcome contribution to the life of the islands?"

"Well, I remember doing a calving on one of Shetland's rare warm summer days. It was a tough one and I was 'glistening' badly so I took off my calving gown and finished the job in my very damp, sleeveless T-shirt. When I was done I turned round and found I had a very appreciative audience of five men – there was the farmer, a couple of farmhands, the postman and a bloke who had just been passing by. There was also a collie romancing my wellies, if that counts."

"You mentioned you had a dog? Is that the yappy – though undoubtedly lovely – Samoyed I've met, Tosca?"

"How dare you! No, it wasn't Tosca, it was a different Tosca – Tosca's father. On my first trip home from Shetland I asked his breeder if I could borrow him to keep me company when I went back. He'd just been retired from being a show dog and he'd never really learned to play or just run about. In Shetland he had the time of his life, going with me on farm visits or on the cliffs watching whales and seals or all the nesting puffins and gannets. We watched the Aurora Borealis one night – fantastic. He came in very useful as a duvet as well. I was 'whited out' in a blizzard one time, up near Esha Ness, and we just curled up together in the car and waited to be rescued."

"I didn't know Esha Ness was a place. I just know it as the answer to a pub quiz question."

"I did have one problem with Tosca right at the beginning. Basically he was a city dog and didn't know how to behave with farm animals. On my very first farm visit, as soon as he was out of the van, he was off after the sheep. The farmer was all right about it, amazingly, but told me he could cure him so he wouldn't have to be kept in the van all the time. He put Tosca in a pen with a ram who gave him a lesson in sheep etiquette, and he was fine after that. But they're really hardy, Shetland ewes. They seem to live on air, not grass. And they're quite small. Farmers used to ask for me as the 'wife vet' for lambings because I had smaller hands."

"I knew Shetland ponies were small. I didn't know it was catching."

"They have their own distinctive stock up there, like bonsai versions of the real thing. You know what Shetland ponies look like? But they're hard as nails and incredibly strong. I was trying to examine one and thought I could control it by holding onto its halter. I got dragged right across the field, sliding through the cow pats. Even Shetland cattle are smaller than you expect and you think they're going to be placid and biddable – until one kicks you."

"I'm sure, in your position, I would have viewed such enriching experiences as learning opportunities."

"Well, my best near-death learning opportunity was when I was called out one night to a Highland cow, brought over from the mainland. It had developed what they call transit fever. It's a kind of stress-induced pneumonia. The cow was in an outhouse with no electricity and just part of a roof. The floor was covered with debris from where the roof had fallen in. It was dark and the cow simply attacked me. You know what they look like with those photogenic designer horns? Well, it tried to gore me with those and when I fell on my back, it got down and tried to crush me with its head. There were two people hitting its head with pitchforks and pulling its horns to try to get it off me while someone else pulled me out."

"If they ever make a film of this, I'm not sure about the 'hitting its head with pitchforks' bit."

"Ok. They could include the bit when I was knocked out by semen instead."

"?"

"You know they use straws of frozen bull semen stored in liquid nitrogen to inseminate cows artificially when farmers don't have their own bulls? I'd been out to a remote croft to see a cow which had just come into season and managed to turn my clapped out old van over on the way back – vets are very good at that. I was hit on the head by the canister containing the frozen semen straws. I was taken to hospital. That's what they wrote on the card at the end of my bed 'concussed by semen'."

"I'm saying absolutely nothing."

"Then there was the time I was transporting some PTS bodies – that's Put to Sleep – in the van. I'd tied the back doors together with baler twine. You see baler twine everywhere in Shetland. The islands are held together with baler twine. Anyway, it must have come loose, because I found I'd been dropping dead dogs and cats in cremation bags at intervals along the main road in Lerwick. I'd lost four or five before I spotted one in the rear view mirror. Had to reverse back down the road to pick them all up. That could have been a bit embarrassing. But then a girl I knew from my vet course in Edinburgh told me there was a vacancy for a locum in a good practice in Northumberland. I applied and got the job..."

"...and started working for my brother."

CHAPTER FOUR

POORER PEOPLE'S PETS

"You enter into a certain amount of madness when you marry a person with pets

Nora Ephron, 1941 - 2012

"Reproduction isn't as simple now as it was when I was a student"

Veterinary obstetrics lecture, 1978

Eventually Margaret decided to give up her job in Morpeth and continue the general migration southwards that she had started in Shetland. She got a new job in Manchester. John, as one of the partners in the Morpeth vet practice, wasn't impressed that I'd stolen his assistant.

The new job turned out to be in Old Trafford with the People's Dispensary for Sick Animals, or PDSA, a charity that employs vets to provide health care for pets whose owners can't afford the vet bills. Initially the "means test" involved little more than asking the client "Can you afford to pay?" Later this changed to requiring evidence that the owner was in receipt of some social welfare benefit, but even then it was sometimes hard to avoid a suspicion that the system was being "worked".

Margaret saw one dog in her consulting room with a home address in the pleasant suburban road where I lived. The "impoverished" dog owner's house was easily identified by the impressive boat occupying the front garden. It transpired that the family dog actually belonged (allegedly) to the student son living at that address and thus qualified for PDSA support. So that was all right then.

One regular and reliable source of charitable income arose from the surgery's location in Old Trafford, close to both the Lancashire county cricket ground and Manchester United's stadium and possessing some handy car parking spaces. Knowing they were United fans made it all the more satisfying, collecting "voluntary" contributions to the PDSA coffers.

Margaret found the work at the PDSA varied and interesting. In truth, once you've spent an hour or so conscientiously picking maggots from a fly-blown rabbit's rear passage, you do welcome variety. Although she found that she missed some of the work with farm ("large") animals that she'd experienced elsewhere, in Shetland and Northumberland, she really didn't miss heading out into muddy fields in the middle of the night for lambings and calvings.

She found herself quite soon appearing in a short documentary about the PDSA for the local television channel. We still have it recorded somewhere on old-fashioned tape but we know from memory that the best bit of a slightly wooden performance comes when Margaret, during a consultation with a patient and in answer to the question "What is it, then?", announces thoughtfully to the screen that it's a "warty outgrowth of the skin". Where did that come from? Anyway, not a phrase she's likely to forget any time soon as her work colleagues manage to slip it into professional conversations with her on a roughly daily basis, nearly twenty years later.

The Mighty Reds are never far from this story. I had a season ticket, or something similar, at Anfield for over twenty years, from around 1972, the journey from my home in Manchester being a short one. And this commitment gave me some priority when it came to seeking tickets for major events like cup finals (those were the days!) I followed the Lads to European Cup Finals at Wembley, Paris and, in May 1985, Brussels, where the venue – the Heysel stadium – has become infamous. Thirty-nine football fans, mainly Italians supporting Juventus, perished when a wall collapsed following fighting between the two sets of supporters. Blame may be reasonably attributed to the supporters of both teams, to some "previous" between English and Italian fans, to the state of the stadium and to the various authorities, but it left one numb and despairing. This ill-starred match, which I attended with my brother, fell just nine days before my wedding and, in the days before mobile phones and instant communication, Margaret heard nothing from me until I arrived home the following morning. We Liverpool fans had been kept isolated after the game in our coaches on the Brussels airport runway and we probably knew less about the fatalities than those watching at home.

The wedding itself was memorable mainly through Margaret's father, responsible for delivering the bride, getting lost on the way both to the Stockport registry office and subsequently to the reception – the latter while convoying behind my own father, thus ensuring that no parents at all turned up at the hotel until a couple of hours after the rest of us. The first official photographs at the reception, taken outdoors quickly before the rain came, are notable for the happy couple being surrounded, in the absence of any parents, by people we don't recognise but who are, one presumes, either distant cousins or hotel staff kindly making up the numbers.

A vet practice, and especially a charitable one, can of course prove to be a magnet for unwanted pets, and Margaret did succumb on more than one occasion to the sad plight of some abandoned creature which she would generously bring home to me - much as one might hand over a new sweater, but with additional feeding responsibilities.

Kenny Bunny, or KB, was the first of these. Named for Liverpool FC legend Kenny Dalglish, he occupied in theory a hutch and a sizeable run that I constructed in the back garden. However, as well as enjoying daily access to the whole of the garden and designing and constructing his own network of tunnels through the lawn, he spent much of the time in the lounge, chewing through TV wires to the shock of both of us, poking his head through huge holes he'd made in the curtains and, in a move which I never failed to find deeply impressive, skilfully lowering his ears when approaching the horizontal struts in chairs. Holding a Malteser between my thumb and index finger while he nibbled it away without making contact was really cool, and even better was the fact that he clearly felt it ungentlemanly conduct to poo indoors.

The next "rescue" kindly brought home by Margaret was Hilda, a mallard duckling found wandering in Manchester city centre and handed into the PDSA. We placed her in the run with KB and she immediately imprinted on him – she assumed Kenny was her mother, father and protector all rolled into one. She worshipped him. Wherever he moved, she hurried to catch up and settled down alongside. When Kenny was allowed to come into the lounge, Hilda, having, unlike the rabbit, a complete absence of bowel control, was left outside in a distraught state, running up and down the length of the picture window until her beloved was returned to her. It was hard to establish Kenny's feelings in the matter. He spoke little and rarely gave anything away.

We knew of course that this situation couldn't last forever and needed to break the news to Hilda that her inability to effect even the simplest hop was down to her innate duckness. A mirror was placed in the run so that, as a self-respecting female, she could check herself out. A tape of bird noises was acquired. We spoke to people we knew who looked after the local country park with its own wildfowl population and persuaded them to accept Hilda from us.

We were as prepared as we could be when, as is the way with

these things, fate played its hand. Late one evening Margaret stepped out into the garden and, in the dark, as good as trod on Hilda, who was at the time enjoying a quiet constitutional round the lawn with Kenny. The duck, never having previously flown so much as a foot off the ground, took off with a squawk of fright and was never seen again, at least not by us. After all our careful preparation this was not the scenario that we had envisaged. Her inaugural flight was made at night into a world which we had not yet mapped nor briefed her on. We did the only sensible thing we could do – we rapidly filled the small paddling pool, acquired solely for Hilda's benefit, and illuminated it by leaving all the house lights on overnight in case she should try to return home. We could but hope that any natural instincts which she might possess and her undoubted good condition might serve her well while she navigated the southern suburbs of Manchester in search of a decent warren.

Piseag (pronounced Peeshek) joined the household soon after. She was – let's be honest here – an ugly and unappealing kitten, but that didn't excuse whoever dumped her outside the PDSA in a bag. We took her into our home and, as Margaret was at that time attending Gaelic language classes (did I mention she's Scottish in the same kind of way that Ian Paisley is Protestant?) she was named after the Gaelic word for kitten. Or it might have been the word for table, or putty – Margaret missed a few classes, you understand.

Piseag had a strange and intense fascination for liquid, whether static or mobile. If I was in the bath she would climb onto the rim to get a close-up view, teeter round the edge and occasionally fall in. Few things in the world were more life-enhancing to Piseag than to observe me "having a wee". (Let me say straight away that there was – and remains - nothing remotely unusual about this process). She would rush to join me in the loo, rise onto her hind legs and peer closely into the "pan" to witness this remarkable event. Unfortunately, and despite my best efforts, it was sometimes impossible to prevent her head coming between me and the target area. Piseag, I'm so sorry, that's all I can say.

But she did possess a more socially acceptable party trick which never let you down. If you picked up a small ball she would rush to the nearest wall and take up a goalkeeping position. If you then bounced the ball towards her, she would leap – honestly, I'm not kidding here – to claw it away before it could hit the wall. This was such a reliable performance that you could confidently show off to visitors with it. Inevitably, if there was a mishap or misjudgement and she got a faceful of ball, she did that cat thing where they shrug and wander off and pretend that was always what had been intended. Until the next time. We used to call this game Grobbelaar after the Liverpool goalkeeper and legend. There was never a suggestion that she might consider putting in anything less than her optimal performance. Or walk on her hands for that matter.

Her gaze would occasionally come to rest unnervingly somewhere over my left shoulder. I might think I was communicating satisfactorily with the cat, only to get the distinct impression that she was actually in touch with some invisible presence behind me. I sometimes found myself turning to check. But whoever or whatever it was, it was always left to us more tangible life forms to deal with the mundane things like supplying her Felix and cat litter.

She took a great interest in her surroundings and liked to accompany us to the shops, following us to the car, leaping in and spending the journey with her back feet on the rear seat and her front paws resting on the back of the driver's seat while peering over my shoulder.

In the end it was the proverbial curiosity that killed her while still very young. Workmen had been digging up the road outside the house and she had been observing them all day from as close a viewing position as she could manage. She was, according to one of the men, checking over their work at the end of the day when a car hit her.

This left our tortoiseshell Purdey temporarily as the household's distraught only cat. Named as a tribute to my favourite Avenger (and later champion of Gurkhas), Purdey was at all times unbearably cute, timid and ladylike. Not this time a PDSA rescue but acquired from a local TV reporter in Manchester whom we knew socially, Purdey spent her early months pretending not to be there, pressing herself face first into the corner of the room. Her first discovery that there was a world outside the house was an absolute entertainment as she put one tentative paw out of the patio door onto the paving and recoiled in horror at finding it wet. It was to take several more days of cautious probing before she was prepared to trust all four paws to be outdoors at the same time.

Meanwhile our rabbit numbers had grown and Kenny had been joined by two youngsters, Sammy, named after another Liverpool FC legend, Sammy Lee, and Chloe, who wasn't. Unlike the unfailingly mild-mannered Kenny, the new arrivals had a degree of "attitude" and declared the enclosed back garden to be their "manor", obliging the cats to live at altitude, sprinting from the sanctuary of the house to scale the garden wall and away.

When our (human) baby, Mairi, arrived, I thought it would help the cats to adjust to the new arrival if I introduced them properly. Little guidance was to be found on this in the parenting manuals. With nervy Purdey clearly agitated by the continuing sounds of crying coming from the cot in the corner of the room, I scooped her up and held her over the cot for a clear sight. Whether Purdey came to believe at that moment that she was about to be fed to the mewling beast below, I do not know, but my arms bore for several years the signs of her flight. She was to spend the remainder of her 19 years convinced that evil was never far away and made it quite clear that allowing this presence into her house was a terrible mistake that should be rectified as soon as was practical.

With Purdey obviously missing Piseag, it wasn't long before the PDSA came up with a replacement. This was in the form of Bridget the Midget, one of a litter of nondescript black and white kittens which had, believe it or not, been bagged and dropped into the River Irwell before being swiftly lifted out by a passer-by. We fed the new arrival by means of a dropper and she soon overcame her difficult start in life.

While Purdey could "cute" for England, Bridget was, frankly, a minger. Purdey favoured the finer things in life, or at least those that emerged from a tin bearing a brand name that she recognised: Bridget, when not meowing loudly from the kitchen to herald the arrival of the latest addition to her unrivalled fir cone collection, would be laying out a nice line in mouse gall bladders for me to stand on.

If you've ever spent time in a car with the windows closed and a cat whose bowels have just given way and abandoned any sense of responsibility, you may have sympathy for me. Bridget needed one day to be transported to Margaret's place of work and I foolishly attempted this feat without the aid of a cat basket. As 95 per cent of her clients have said over the years, it's well-nigh impossible to get the little sods in there, and it's just as difficult to get them out at the other end. So, a frightened Bridget was making the journey on the loose, as it were, which would also, as it happens, describe her bodily functions, which were all pervasive and frankly would have been unacceptable in polite society. Tempting though it was to encourage her to flee at 40 mph through an open window, I settled for driving at an improper speed by the most direct route to the surgery in the hope that any cat-owning magistrate would understand where I was coming from. It was also tricky explaining away in my office the appalling state of my brown-stained mileage claim form which lay on the rear seat, protecting the upholstery from further punishment.

I frequently questioned why I was paying for the privilege

of housing and feeding a creature that simply didn't like me. While Bridget had what appeared to be an adoring relationship with Margaret, the cat and I tended to tread warily in each other's presence, suspecting each other's motives and behaviours. It is true that I did once manage to slam the bathroom door on her tail and she made a most unearthly noise by way of response, but I mean, come on, get over it. I vividly recall lying on my back on the sofa in front of a television documentary when Bridget suddenly leapt up to stand on my chest and peer at me. The tension on both sides was palpable. Reluctant, to put it mildly, to make any sudden move that might be misconstrued, I managed without moving my torso to text unobtrusively to my wife upstairs, beseeching her to come at all speed to my rescue.

She didn't improve with age (Bridget, that is) and developed an array of off-putting, if medically benign, tumours on back and head which discouraged any desire I might otherwise have shown for physical contact. That, and the tendency if stroked, to hold her tail bolt upright and thrust her pencil sharpener into your face.

Both Purdey and Bridget were to live into their twentieth year before Margaret – not known as the Terminator, or the Angel of Death, for nothing – felt it necessary to call a humane end to proceedings. Perhaps it says something that, while Purdey was treated to a private cremation at a local pet sanctuary and a ceremonial scattering of her ashes in the back garden (though she would have been appalled by the thought of making the journey home from the crematorium in a Tupperware box), I saved money on Bridget and dug her a hole behind the pond.

The lack of a financial deterrent for PDSA clients could be a problem at night time. Working in his own mixed veterinary practice in Morpeth, my brother at least had the option of saying to nocturnal callers, "OK, I can come out if it's really an emergency, but it'll be at least £50 for the initial callout. Sorry, what? It'll wait? You're sure? OK, bring it down to the surgery in the morning." This of course didn't apply at the PDSA as the clients weren't paying, so the vet had to develop the skill to identify what really did justify getting out of bed and driving a dozen miles for, and what didn't.

In those dark and distant times before mobile phones ruined our nights, we used to take a pager to bed with us and, when alerted, were required to call back for details to the independent answering service which provided unsocial hours phone coverage for vets (and equivalent professions, like plumbers). But the impact on my REMs when the beeper beeped was as nothing compared with the tension I felt waiting for Margaret to follow me into wakefulness. This at 3 am from the pager: "Good morning Beeper 828" (funny how you never forget the number), "I have one message for you. There's a Thai water dragon with its lip stuck to the side of its tank. Could you ring the owner please on..." And later the same night, "There's a dog won't come out from under the wardrobe and the owner would like some advice from you..." My other half can demonstrate a rich and varied vocabulary at any time of day. In the wee small hours it could take on a hue all of its own.

Once we'd made contact with the anxious nocturnal client,

his or her grasp of the veterinary arrangements would often be limited. They might for example ask if any of the other vets were available "because we usually see that old bloke with the accent". Just how many vets did they think were likely to be sharing our bed at that time of night?

I became reasonably adept at guessing which cases might enable us to turn over and attempt to rejoin the arms of Morpheus and which meant a trip down to the surgery – for all three of us. The PDSA premises were located in a fairly basic part of Old Trafford and Margaret wasn't particularly keen to open up the surgery and its drugs cupboard on her own in the middle of the night. I could have pretended to sleep through the pager and the ensuing phone conversation but she just *knew* and, although she didn't actually insist, it was always understood that she'd be appreciative if I went with her – "though it's entirely up to you, of course".

We had become a family of three a few years after Margaret began working at the PDSA and, from that time onwards, there was an additional consideration in the night. So, with baby still asleep in the carrycot on the rear seat, off we frequently went.

During our early days with the PDSA there were no veterinary nurses on call overnight to assist the duty vet, so I would be roped in to play the part – with no training of course, and no fee. As the expert's unskilled sidekick and hod carrier, I sometimes felt I was performing as Robin to Batman, Debbie McGee to Paul Daniels or, for those of a Reckitt's Blue and Fry's Five Boys generation, Digby to Dan Dare.

While the wife advanced with a needle towards the offending pet, I was the one wrapping the dangerous little chap in a towel and doing my best to hang on with gritted teeth. And, if by any chance the bundle of joy should achieve its ambition, struggle free and succeed in sinking either tooth or claw into the target, guess whose fault that was. There appeared to be no professional guidelines to structure the frank exchange of views which invariably followed.

I will admit that there was a good deal of pleasure – as well as huge relief – to be had from managing to keep an animal safely anaesthetised with Margaret supervising me from the other end while opening it up and doing the clever stuff, and even more at helping to bring slimy live pups out one by one from a caesarean.

Once the more old-fashioned clients had established that, despite clearly being the male, I wasn't actually the vet and my wife would be taking on the more technical roles for tonight's performance. I in turn became the shoulder to weep on and in a long line of accomplishments I can claim to have satisfactorily consoled large numbers of distraught nocturnal pet owners, including one extended Rastafarian group who were quite overwrought about a poorly spaniel.

I recall Margaret one night gently outlining the process leading up to and including cremation to a bereaved owner, to be answered with the relieved words, "Well, at least they don't just burn them, then."

I was regarded as key adviser on such sensitive issues as whether the newly-terminated pet should be accompanied into doggy afterlife by its collar, blanket or favourite toy. And, though I say it myself, I feel I carried out my duties with some aplomb and quite insufficient recognition.

It is true that there were on occasion other, sometimes unexpected, sources of help. Notably a local transvestite, attractively dressed for an evening out with glossy hair, large hands and visible stubble, well over six feet tall, who, waiting one night to have her/his Pekingese seen by the vet, took exception to the behaviour and language being shown towards Margaret by another client, clearly worse for drink. She seized the offending loudmouth by the throat, warned him about his behaviour and held him firmly against the wall until the police arrived.

I don't recall there being any helpful restrictions on the vet's hours of working, so Margaret might find herself working through the day, being on call through the following night, including perhaps two separate trips down to the surgery in Old Trafford, and back in work the next day. I'm sure my own work performance at the time also varied in line with our night time on-call rota. "No boss, I'm not asleep, I find that resting my forehead on the desk helps me to think through our next environmental campaign."

Of course, pagers weren't only designed as sleep destroyers. Taking ours with us on evenings out, we managed to add colour to more than one play and concert with a surprise jingle, though it was hard to convince ourselves that Aly Bain, the legendary Shetland fiddler, saw our musical input to his work as entirely positive.

Coconut Willy's was Stockport's finest, indeed only,

vegetarian restaurant. This being the 1980s, it was also the first vegetarian place I'd eaten in that seemed to use things like ingredients and recipes – and a chef – rather than just chopping up bits of cabbage. It was New Year's Eve and, demonstrating that I was in touch with my inner "new man", I had booked a table there rather than my usual Chinese. Margaret was on duty for any possible emergency call-outs overnight. We were taking a chance on her work pager not going off and spoiling the evening. "It'll be all right", we said. "It's bound to be quiet at New Year. They'll all be too busy enjoying themselves."

As it happened, not everyone shared our view that the hours before the midnight bells might best be devoted to happy contemplation of the past twelve months and ill-founded optimism for the new year to come. Margaret was paged before the starters, during the main course and again while pretending not to be tempted by the dessert menu. On each occasion she conscientiously, if a tad grumpily, set aside her plate and borrowed the restaurant's landline in the kitchen (we'd been good customers during the year) to call whichever client had contacted the vets' emergency out-of-hours service. She succeeded in grouping all the deserving cases for one post-prandial trip to the surgery.

As he heard the pager beep for the fourth time during the evening, the waiter, who was bearing our puddings at that moment through the swing door from the kitchen, spun on his heel without a word and disappeared back the way he'd come. Exactly what passed through his mind a few moments later on hearing the other half enquire over the phone near the chopping board, "And can you describe the motions? Is there blood in the stools?" we shall never know. We tipped quite well that evening.

So, dining at home, that's the answer. Well, possibly not. At least, not on Christmas Day. Not when yours truly, performing his annual party piece by assembling the world's finest turkey roast with trimmings (including, I'm bound to say, a rather excellent bread sauce), has been slaving all morning, only to have it sabotaged by some client with dubious pet management skills. When the vet has to set off between mouthfuls of sprout, absentmindedly still wearing her paper hat, to visit the second canine of the day that's been carried in comatose with chocolate poisoning, having broken into the jumbo-sized bars under the tree and added a jar of Quality Street for good measure, and I'm reduced to trying to pull a cracker with the baby in the pushchair, I know it's not my day.

So, with Margaret content at the PDSA, me happy at Greater Manchester Council, living in a city we liked and with a good social life, what could possibly go wrong?

Margaret Thatcher, that's what.

CHAPTER FIVE

A LIFE IN PIGS:
THE ABATTOIR YEARS

*"Dogs look up to us, Cats look down on us.
Pigs treat us as equals"*

Sir Winston Leonard Spencer Churchill KG etc, 1874 – 1965

*"Lamb dysentery is found in areas where
there are sheep"*

Veterinary medicine lecture, 1978

Ken Livingstone eventually worked his way too far under Margaret Thatcher's skin and the result was the abolition not only of the Greater London Council but of the other metropolitan county councils, including the one I worked for – Greater Manchester Council, or GMC. No evidence was put forward in Greater Manchester in terms of poor service delivery, lack of democratic accountability or financial mismanagement to justify the turmoil this created. We weren't the target. I think we were what is known as collateral damage.

The period leading up to the day of Abolition in 1986 proved, for those of us employed at County Hall, traumatic on a number of levels.

Dedicated staff strove throughout the last two years of the council's existence to bring to fruition important projects that had been in gestation and might otherwise be lost – you know, saving the planet, that sort of thing - but in a political climate of hostility between central and local government that threw up barriers at every turn. I'm sure it happens in any political or economic crisis, but I witnessed colleagues disintegrating under the pressure, marriages breaking up and even a colleague from my own department dying in the building, all apparently attributable at least in part to the stress. Margaret Thatcher and I were never likely to be friends, but this issue alone would be enough to keep us apart for a few decades at least.

Arrangements were made to maintain some key elements of the work of the disappearing County Council. Some staff left for other parts of the country, others were taken onto the books of the metropolitan district councils which would remain in place, while others left the public sector and took their redundancy pay to set up their own businesses.

Leaving dos became an important consideration. If you were one of the first to flee County Hall, two years ahead of Abolition day, you probably benefited from the usual office whip-round, or collection envelope and card to sign (Best Wishes for the Future, Good Luck with Your New Job/House/Partner, We'll Miss You, Don't Do Anything I Wouldn't Do, Who Are You

Again?), and had your own lunchtime session in the pub. As time went on, however, you might begin to suspect that you could be the last one left to turn off the lights, with nobody to put anything into your envelope. However, as one last political gesture to annoy Mrs T, the Labour-controlled County Council diverted cash into an Abolition party to be held at the Liverpool Road (Station) Museum of Science and Industry. If I didn't get round to it before, and you were a Greater Manchester ratepayer in 1986, can I just say thanks for all the beer and Twiglets that night, it was great. Though I regretted it next day.

Easter happened to coincide that year with the end of March and the day of GMC's Abolition. While most of my colleagues would be starting new jobs elsewhere after Easter, I was due to return to a near-empty County Hall in charge of one of the small units kept together to continue some of the work of GMC. The team would now be accountable not to one county council but to a joint committee of the ten metropolitan city and district councils across Greater Manchester, like Bolton, Stockport and Tameside.

After working for GMC from its first day in 1974 till its last in 1986 and having endured the difficult last two years under the threat of Abolition, I felt in need of, and entitled to, some form of "punctuation mark" before returning to work in the same building after the break. So, with two colleagues, I did the only sensible thing and headed for a long weekend in Belfast – during the annual commemoration of the Easter uprising. The first hotel we phoned had to turn us down on the grounds that they'd "taken a bit of a bomb" the previous week. We drew lots for whose car we went in. I lost.

Having spent my working career embedded in a large bureaucracy, it was odd to return to County Hall after the Easter break with the tumbleweed already beginning to roll down the corridors. I had sixteen staff to manage in the new Greater Manchester Countryside Unit, but no toilet rolls, biros or stamps. I soon sent search parties round the building roped together, on the lookout for any other survivors, furniture, computers, crisps, indeed anything that might come in useful. Come the apocalypse, I'll have a head start.

Margaret (Ankers, not Thatcher) also had a change of job round about this time. My brother, you may recall, had set out to establish himself in the first practice that employed him in Northumberland. He was to remain with that practice throughout his career, acquiring a partner's share in the business, which involved recruiting and employing other vets, some of whom, including his son, Sam, were to become partners in their turn. Even as senior partner in recent years, John has been able to continue seeing clients and deploying his veterinary skills and training, but he has also been involved, with other members of his family, in running a major business, with all that entails. There are premises, extremely expensive equipment and supplies to maintain; staff to recruit, induct, train and manage; health and safety and other legal requirements to be met; risk assessments to be carried out; drugs to be ordered, finances to be husbanded. When a client mutters that their pet only had an injection or a prescription and complains about the cost, it will be these unavoidable business costs that they overlook.

Margaret never set her eyes on the same career plan. From the outset she knew she was keen on the vetting bit but not really on the business part, and she always intended that there would be other dimensions to her life unrelated to animals and their owners. John, as we will see, certainly developed some major, consuming interests outside the vet business – but most of them were still very much livestock orientated!

Margaret hadn't been particularly happy about having to drop our daughter at nursery each day because she was working full time. Mairi had learned to call out "Bye, see you Monday" in a strong Mancunian accent whenever she parted company with anybody, at any stage of the week, which I thought was rather nice. What eventually did it for Margaret was collecting her one afternoon and watching her proudly hold the hand of a nursery nurse and take her first steps unsteadily but deliberately down the hall to the front door. That evening a visibly-upset Margaret, appalled that she hadn't been the one to facilitate this landmark event, determined to find another job, one that would enable her to spend at least part of the week with her toddler.

With no part-time work available with local vet practices, that new job turned out, unexpectedly, to be in an abattoir and cutting plant on the east side of Manchester.

The pay was good. The shift work hours involved starting at four or five in the morning, but that meant she was often free by the middle of the day. The job was Official Veterinary

Surgeon, responsible for overseeing and certifying not only animal welfare but meat hygiene, and little could happen in that plant without the blessing of the OVS.

This particular plant handled only pigs. The responsibilities of the OVS ran from the arrival at the plant of live animals, checking for any injuries, signs of suffering and disease significant to human health, through to the policing of slaughter and staff hygiene practices, and certification of meat for export.

While I may have found Margaret's change of kit to clipboard, white wellies, white coat and helmet rather fetching, there was no doubt that the assorted slaughtermen and pig-stickers tended to regard her as something of a threat who could potentially bring the lines to a halt, have a man sacked and cost the firm many thousands of pounds if she detected a failure in the humane stunning or killing processes. It was a distinctly male, and frequently hostile, environment.

She undoubtedly found the work depressing and to some extent dehumanising. It was repetitive, focused on checklists and form stamping, and something of a waste of her years of veterinary training. Our dinner party conversations now featured words like debristling and exsanguination, and the distinctive aroma of uncooked pork hung everywhere in the air, on clothes and hair when she arrived home from work.

The experience brought about some changes in family habits. With Margaret setting a 3 am alarm and consequently wanting early nights and me still on normal office hours, we tended to pass one another on the landing and communicate through grunts and written notes – much as we do now, come to think of it.

Margaret found (and to some extent finds to this day) that the smell of pigs and pork products tends to cling to you, and the routine of watching a succession of live animals turn into prime cuts before her eyes brought her close, though not all the way, to vegetarianism. She had been down this route towards vegetarianism a few years earlier, following a visit to an Edinburgh abattoir organised as part of a module in public health and hygiene on her veterinary course, and had been outraged one day to spot her mother surreptitiously grating chicken into her home-made vegetable soup for fear that her daughter wasn't getting enough goodness in her meals.

Margaret never managed to persuade me to turn my back on eating dead animals, but I am obliged to be furtive. One of my first actions if she's going away for a few days is to sneak out to the butcher's for a pile of kidneys to devil – my idea of a guilty weekend. But it's a bit like when I used to smoke cigars when she was away: I have to spend the remainder of the weekend with all the windows open.

A few years later, during the country's outbreak of mad cow disease and the saga of John Gummer's daughter and the hamburger, we caught a ministerial announcement on the telly aimed at providing reassurance about measures being taken to safeguard public health. The spokesman started to say how the nation's slaughtermen, in the front line of Britain's fight against the disease, would be carefully and surgically removing the potentially iffy spinal tissue to prevent any threat to human health. We exchanged glances, remembered the subtle skills and attitudes of Margaret's former colleagues at the abattoir and resolved not to go near beef for a few more years.

Horse flesh now, that's a different matter – that's my subtle link into saying it was around this time that we discovered the sport of trotting, properly known as harness racing, at a rather tired-looking track near Droylsden, on the east side of Manchester. I think the venue was called Carriages, but I have a feeling it's no longer there.

I'm not really a horse person – my chief interest in that direction remains Aintree and the Grand National, which both my wife and daughter disapprove of on horse welfare grounds. But I do know, from having enjoyed a few evenings at Carriages back in the 1980s, that "trotting" involves diagonal pairs of legs moving at the same time, while "pacing" means that the right legs, front and hind, move together, then the left – children, only try this under adult supervision. Or preferably not at all.

The "driver" sits behind on a "sulky", a light two-wheeled cart with bicycle wheels, and they fair shift round the track.

Margaret – the vet, remember – would give me a comprehensive and informed appraisal of each equine entrant as they paraded before the race and I placed my bets with optimism. I don't, however, recall ever actually having to trouble the bookies for any winnings.

Meanwhile I was enjoying my new professional role with the Greater Manchester Countryside Unit, having to demonstrate the team's value to our funding local authorities, the ten metropolitan councils remaining after GMC's abolition. My role included promoting both the Unit and the achievements and aspirations of the ten councils, and I had the opportunity to put in some time with the umbrella group for similar authorities covering the nation's major conurbations, the Association of Metropolitan Authorities or AMA.

With the Conservative party in power nationally and the AMA being largely Labour controlled, I was occasionally drafted in by the latter to bring our GMCU team's expertise to bear on topical issues and prospective legislation. The Environmental Protection Act of 1990 was a case in point and required me to attend committee stages on the bill in both Lords and Commons. One reading of the bill in the House of Lords clashed with England's (football) World Cup semi-final tie against (West) Germany, which was a bit of a downer – though I may have used a different word at the time. I tried to put the football out of my mind as I sat in the advisers' "box" behind the Labour peers, casually picking cat hairs from my only suit and scribbling and passing briefing notes for all I was worth as the debate proceeded. On the opposite, government, side there was a team of civil servants doing the same thing. On our side, there was, erm, me.

At one point during the evening a friendly Andrew McIntosh came over for a word. That's Baron McIntosh of Haringey and he was leading the debate for the Opposition (look, I'm sorry about the name-dropping thing but that's who it was and we were in the House after all, that's just who you get there). He explained that the debate was adjourning for a short while and would I prefer to go for a quick bite or "join some of the lads" in the TV lounge to catch part of the game? I happily took the second option, thinking "You don't get to do this too often", and followed some friendly earl or other.

Sadly we were all recalled to resume the debate in the House before the footy action had ended but, through the next hour or so, were kept up to speed by a succession of peers of the realm approaching the Bar of the House and signalling the latest score, including the subsequent penalty shoot-out, which was, inevitably, won by the Germans.

And, talking of the 1990 Environmental Protection Act as we were (and that's a line you don't want to read too often), I lay confident claim to having made one of the few public jokes about Part VI of the Act, on "the definition of a regime of statutory notification and risk assessment for genetically modified organisms". We'd not really heard of GMOs before 1990. The legislation covered a bit of a ragbag of environmental issues, mainly related to the safe handling of waste (no, stay with me). The AMA (see above, I'm not going to explain again) organised a full day's workshop on the provisions in the bill while it was going through Parliament, dealing with each Part in turn, and I was invited to participate. Following discussion on Part VI and GMO's we naturally enough reached my bit, Part VII, about the reorganisation of the government's rural agencies, in a kind of death slot just before the long awaited lunch break.

I began my remarks "When I was a little lad my mother once gave me this piece of sound advice, 'Stephen', she said, 'whatever else you do in life, make sure you never come between a genetically-modified organism and its lunch' and this is advice I have always, until today, taken to heart".

It worked better live.

Though the work was fun, I had become aware, through the trauma of GMC's demise, that nothing could be taken for granted employment-wise. I started to keep an eye out for relevant vacancies in the jobs pages of *The Guardian* and was invited to a number of interviews, mainly in national parks across the country. I've been rejected in some of the nicest places – Dartmoor, Brecon Beacons, Exmoor, the Yorkshire Dales, the Broads. At least they usually put me up in a pleasant hotel for a night or two between their series of interviews and tests before turning me down in favour of the in-house candidate.

Naturally I would put in plenty of preparation, trying to anticipate the kind of questioning that might arise and putting my faith in the principle that, as we were talking about a national asset, the members of the National Park Authority would be keen to explore with me just how we might encourage more of the impoverished urban populations of the North and Midlands to come to visit and stay. So it would be disappointing to find that a farming member of the interviewing panel only wanted to test me on whether I knew the names of his fields.

At the Exmoor interview I didn't feel things had gone well over the three days of the process. I felt they didn't like me any more than I took to them and, in truth, I was looking forward to going home. So, when we got round to the final interview and I was asked what I thought about conserving the local tradition of stag hunting, I told them.

I didn't get the job. My guess is it went to the in-house candidate.

Wait, there's more.

A month or two later, still employed in the Greater Manchester Countryside Unit, I hosted a visit to the city by a senior staff member of the Countryside Commission, the government advisory body on rural matters at that time. We hadn't met before and I introduced myself to him at the railway station. "Ah yes," he said, "I hope you weren't too disappointed at not getting the Exmoor job? I believe you gave the interview panel the benefit of your views on stag hunting?"

It was probably a year after this that I found myself in Norwich being interviewed for a top post at the Broads Authority. "Mr Ankers", said the first questioner from Norfolk County Council, "I understand you hold particularly interesting views on stag hunting..."

Meanwhile, in Northumberland, my brother and his family were settling well into a rural lifestyle and had relocated their home from the county town of Morpeth to a farm on the edge of the nearby village of Longhorsley. On one of my early visits I noticed a house in the village bearing a plaque; early last century it had been the family home of Emily Wilding Davison. Emily, it will be remembered, was a suffragette who was killed when she grappled with King George V's horse, Anmer, in the 1913 Epsom Derby – with the return half of her rail ticket famously still in her pocket. Either, one may assume, she didn't intend suicide or the arcane nature of rail pricing meant that an anytime super Edwardian off-peak single would have cost more. Longhorsley and Morpeth hosted a programme of events in 2013 to mark the centenary of Emily's most celebrated moment of direct action.

As well as being a key partner in a large veterinary practice, based in Morpeth but spawning branch surgeries in towns around, John, Shelagh and their children Nicky and Sam set about transforming a complex of farm buildings which was centred on their attractive traditional farmhouse of yellowish Northumbrian sandstone. They inherited with the farm a long established civil defence and early warning station – essentially an underground bunker which was, a few years later, given up by the government in Whitehall once the Russians had promised not to attack. The bunker didn't really offer scope for much in the way of guided tours or a heritage experience, but local kids seemed to make their own entertainment down there before John sealed it up.

Substantial tree and hedge planting took place around the farm perimeter and field boundaries and, with John being a confirmed "birder", opportunities were taken to improve the wildlife habitats.

Dog numbers on the farm steadily grew, often pets unwanted by previous owners. Cats, rabbits and other "normal" pets arrived and thrived in the spacious surroundings along with tanks full of tropical fish, terrapins and as many as thirty tortoises. I spent one weekend, when visiting, helping to construct and plant up a linked series of aviaries, to be occupied by various exotic pheasants, hornbills and quail. Ponds were excavated and soon populated with ducks, geese and various other wildfowl. Snow-white doves fluttered and cooed around the outbuildings and the farmyard.

On a semi-commercial but probably loss-making basis the family raised rare varieties of sheep and cattle, contributing to their conservation and regularly winning rosettes at Highland and other country shows. This may have been an expensive pastime but at least the vet bills were manageable. Over the years, as the hobby element of the enterprise grew, they created paddocks to house wallabies, emus, llamas and rheas. I learned not to be too soft when dealing with some of these livestock. When a bad-tempered male llama starts to bring volumes of green bile up its throat, it's time to start putting some distance between you, and when it makes a serious effort to mount you, immediate and active discouragement is called for, through the medium of a clenched fist, rather than, say, drafting a stiff memo.

I always enjoyed an excuse to drive the quad bike round the fields, only ending up underneath it once – where, I maintain, the remains of a hedge had been insufficiently grubbed out. We discovered that many of the animals had been named, which I always believed (erroneously, as it happens) made it difficult to eat them later. My mother had been recognised by having a nanny goat named after her; even David Campese, the Australian rugby player, had a wallaby named in his honour. On enquiring, we learned that a pair of Vietnamese potbellied pigs had been named Steve and Margaret as a friendly family tribute to John's only sibling, which was nice, with the new piglets designated Mairi 1, Mairi 2, Mairi 3, Mairi 4 and Mairi 5. Our daughter pronounced this "well good" and definitely one in the eye for her primary school friends back home.

Visiting Uncle John's farm was of course an absolute joy for our young one. Kitted out in her own miniature farm overalls, mixing and delivering feedstuffs to the livestock grazing in the fields and feeding lambs from two bottles simultaneously, proved the sort of holiday experience one can usually only dream about. Coming down to the kitchen in the morning to find the Aga providing life-saving warmth to one or more abandoned lambs or draped with the occasional makeshift pouch containing an abandoned "joey", or baby wallaby, also tends to add interest to a child's visit to her relatives.

On Easter Sunday morning she was taken round the hen coops to collect eggs for the family breakfast, only to discover that, amazingly, some of the birds had laid eggs made entirely of chocolate.

Christmas was something else again. We had always been one of those families that liked to "big up" the whole Santa Claus thing – partly for our daughter, mainly for me - but, on Uncle John's farm, we were in full fantasy land. Not only did Rudolph leave teeth marks in the carrots for inspection on Christmas morning, but he and his chums had conveniently left distinctive reindeer poo in the yard and sleigh tracks in the snow still lying on the outhouse roofs. So well did this experience reinforce the traditional Santa story over the years that we felt obliged to break the awful truth to Mairi before she went off to university.

We have so many other happy Christmas memories from the farm, not least the year when John had acquired half a dozen peacocks which, apparently, need time to familiarise themselves with new surroundings. Carrying out a stock check round the farm after the usual huge festive dinner on Christmas Day, and just as it started to go dark (soon after noon, it seemed, that far north), John reported back to a slumped and moribund family that the peacocks had gone walkabout – or an aerial equivalent – and needed to be lured back to the relative security of the farm before night fell and left them at the mercy of the local fox population. Struggling to overcome the inevitable effects of double helpings of roast turkey and the rest of the trimmings (my family doesn't do modest portions at Christmas), washed down with white wine and probably, in my case, a little dessert wine for the pudding, the men of the house lumbered out into the gloom. My abiding memory of the next hour or so is of Uncle Al, a South African originally but living in Niagara Falls and married to Shelagh's sister, perched high up a horse chestnut tree still wearing the paper hat from his cracker, glass of brandy in one hand and with a cigar clamped between his teeth, defying gravity to lean way out towards the next tree along and prod at a recalcitrant peacock with a pole. It beats post-prandial Monopoly anyway.

Becoming familiar with farming and adept at using and driving a full range of agricultural machinery led John's daughter, Nicky, to supplement her income one summer by helping out on one or two farms nearby. It has often been said that a farm can be the most dangerous working environment, especially now that numbers employed have decreased so much that one can find oneself isolated while in charge of a potentially lethal weapon. One day Nicky was lowering the back of a tractor trailer when it trapped her arm. In the most extreme pain, she couldn't move, was starting to feel worryingly faint and her cries for help could not be heard above the continuing sound of the tractor. She remained in this horrifying state for almost an hour until, by removing and throwing her boots over a wall, she was at last able to attract attention.

Nicky's arm had been almost severed and she went through a lengthy and traumatic succession of operations to reattach its component parts. Her embryonic career as a physiotherapist looked for a long time to be threatened but, with the passage of time, and displaying a good deal of fortitude, she has eventually been able to make an almost complete recovery and a successful return to work.

If one creature may be said to be the quintessence of John's farm, the single beast that the devisers of local treasure hunts could confidently rely on, the fill-in subject of regional television reports whenever news was slow, it would have to be Gloria, the camel.

Gloria – a single humped dromedary - was the long-term object of Aladdin, the llama's, unrequited lust, permanently separated as they were by two robust hedge lines and a minor road. She had been acquired from a small private zoo in the south west of England and, with a road journey of over 300 miles to the farm, John had asked me if it would be all right for them to break the trip at our new house in the southern suburbs of Stockport to give the camel a decent rest and a walk round. I said I thought this was a completely brilliant idea and just the thing to help us worry our new neighbours.

We were to see plenty of Gloria over the next twenty years on our visits to Northumberland. On one occasion Margaret, glancing out of the bedroom window, was appalled to spot me holding toddler Mairi up to say hello to Gloria in her loose box in the yard. The camel's way of making an acquaintance turned out to involve taking the whole of one's head, or as much as was feasible, between her large, slobbery lips – gently, mind. Don't knock it till you've tried it.

As Mairi grew a little older, being allowed to lead Gloria out of the loose box and across the road into the field became routine. This of course had to be photographed, which came in handy when, during "Show and Tell" at primary school, Mairi's account of looking after the camel (and wallabies, llamas, etc, etc) over the weekend was seriously questioned by teacher.

Gloria always seemed healthy and content in the Northumbrian countryside but she eventually went the way of all flesh and was buried in the field that had been her home. Just so you won't need to ask, there is just the one hump visible now in the ground to mark her passing.

So, with all these wonderful animal options to reflect on, it was something of a surprise that Margaret, entertaining Mairi on the long drive home from the farm, should opt to make up stories about a dolphin called Dominic and a bear named Leonard and all the merry japes they had together. Just how limiting this scenario was became apparent to me when Margaret fell into a deep, fly-catching slumber on the M6 somewhere round Tebay services and Mairi insisted that I take up the narrative mantle. If you can think of a handful of ways in which these lovable pals – dolphin and bear, remember - might best engage with one another, I would be grateful if you could keep them to yourself. But, around twenty years ago, they would have come in very handy.

CHAPTER SIX

GOING TO THE DOGS

"In ancient times cats were worshipped as gods;
they have not forgotten this"

Sir Terry Pratchett OBE

"There's a limit to how long you want to stand about
with an artificial vagina in your hand

Veterinary obstetrics lecture, 1981

Sometimes you just need to move on. We could have stayed contentedly working in the Manchester area amongst friends and in a great city, where I had lived for twenty years and Margaret for ten. But eventually a colleague who knew I was getting itchy feet put in front of me a job advert which he thought might interest me, heading up the environmental work for East Sussex County Council.

The post was based in Lewes, not a place I knew much about other than being one of the smaller county towns. Following a number of failed job attempts in nice places around the country I had taught myself not to build up my hopes, but I was offered an interview. Just before I left the office to head south on the train the evening before, I received a message from my line manager which read, "I don't know if you heard about today's meeting on your team's finances, but if you get offered the Sussex job, you should take it". So, that was all good.

The next day in Lewes I took the opportunity between my interview in the morning and the gathering of the candidates at the end of the afternoon to take a good look round the town, on the basis that there was a fair chance I might never see it again. Over lunch I noticed what looked suspiciously like cat sick on the shoulder of my interview suit and wondered if my job prospects might have been marginally improved had I seen it earlier. I returned to the county council HQ clutching two newly-bought and unfeasibly large cuddly toys for my daughter, a pink pig called Lewis (get it?) who was, sadly, stolen along with the family car shortly afterwards, and an impressively lifelike gorilla, Andrew, who's still a member of the household. Andrew was later to perform noble service, strapped to my wife's saddle on a cycling holiday in Holland and so providing a much-needed cushion for her nether regions, which were glowing brightly enough at night in our hotel room for us to read by. Andrew thought about auditioning for the drumming role in the Cadburys Dairy Milk advert a few years ago, but had a kind of lactose-free thing going on at the time.

East Sussex apparently liked me, I liked them, or it, and twenty years later we're still there. Lewes itself is a brilliant little town that consistently punches above its weight - especially in the criminal world, with the high concentration of murderers and other serious criminals brought before our courts or locked up in our prison. It's a great place to potter round, with its Norman castle, narrow twittens (lanes bordered by continuous high flint walls) and challengingly steep streets, and the picturesque, independent Harveys brewery standing alongside the River Ouse and giving out a splendid (my wife and daughter disagree with me on this one) aroma.

Being "alternative" seems always to have been the Lewes "thing". The barons, led by Simon de Montfort, defeated the army of King Henry III here in 1264, which in my book counts as being a tad left of centre. The Marian persecutions of 1555 to 1557 included the burning at the stake of seventeen Protestant martyrs outside what is now the town hall – an event commemorated each year on 5 November, along with the Gunpowder Plot, in the country's biggest annual bonfire celebrations. In the late 18th century we (we?) were home for several pivotal years to Tom Paine without whom no major political revolution, and certainly not the American or French ones, would have been complete. Interesting to wonder how Tom would get along in modern-day Lewes. Organising petitions about the local parking scheme probably, or picketing pubs which didn't stock Harveys. In true Lewes fashion he has his own beer named after him.

Surprisingly, Lewes – in Sussex, remember - admits to Britain's worst-ever loss of life in an avalanche. Eight people died in 1836 following a major fall of snow from high ground overlooking the eastern end of the town, commemorated in the name of the pub now close to the site – the Snowdrop. On the other hand, we lay claim to the oldest freshwater lido in the country, our own currency (the Lewes pound) and Rodin's "the Kiss". Admittedly this last had to be removed and hidden from public view at the insistence of Miss Fowler-Tutt (honestly), headmistress of the local girls' school. This is going back a bit, mind, to the First World War, when it was feared the statue might give ideas to the large number of young soldiers billeted round the town.

When one of the fiercely-independent rival bonfire societies lost its torches to the river, the other societies stepped in to replace them. The brewery bottled, as "Ouse Booze", the brew that had been interrupted when the site had to be evacuated, and donated the sales to the flood relief fund. With the brewing process having gone on longer than was decent because of the evacuation, the resulting "Booze" put hairs on the chest of the smoothest Lewesian and was likely to lead to further inundation if you walked too close to the river on the way home.

There are of course potential downsides to small-town living. Be very, very careful who you gesticulate at through the car window. That complete and utter plonker who just cut you up may well prove to be a near neighbour, a teacher at your offspring's primary school, a member of your babysitting network or a member of the council committee you will be reporting to later that afternoon. Or in my most memorable case, all of those.

We seem to have more societies than people in Lewes and most of those have plenty to contribute to any debate, any issue. We're also now within the country's newest national park, the South Downs, and if, through bigging the place up in this way, I can contribute to pushing up house prices, then I'm happy to claim credit – or deny any involvement, depending on who's reading this.

It may be appropriate at this stage to point out that, while Liverpool FC had ruled the roost of English and European football throughout the twenty years I had lived and worked in the North West and held a season ticket at the club, I moved south in 1992 and the Reds haven't won the English league title since. I make no specific claim, I merely make the observation.

My final day's work (well, prolonged leaving do, to be honest) with the Greater Manchester Countryside Unit had been on the day after John Major's surprise general election victory in 1992. My wife, herself no great fan of the Conservative Party, and somewhat apprehensive about the next phase of the progression southwards which had so far taken her from Shetland to Northumberland to Greater Manchester, looked with some interest at the swathe of blue across the south of England as depicted in the newspaper's election results map and asked, "So, where are you taking me exactly?"

The answer for the next few months turned out to be "nowhere" as I headed south to Lewes to start the new job and seek out appropriate living accommodation and a suitable primary school for Mairi, while Margaret stayed on to do the fun bits, like selling the house in Stockport.

In Lewes I found, firstly, a convenient B&B and then lodgings with a remarkable octogenarian, vegan homeopath ("I don't mind you bringing meat into the house but I don't want to see it eyeing me up when I open the fridge"). Mrs Thompson's political views were way to the left. She worshipped Tony Benn and invited me during my first few days to accompany her to Lewes' annual Hiroshima commemoration, floating candles down the River Ouse. She also had a nice turn of phrase and I have cheerfully incorporated into my own speech such ejaculations as "What larks!". When offered "Have a nice day" by some young waitress, she was inclined to respond, "Shan't if I don't want to". I miss her.

I was soon to discover that Mrs Thompson was in fact not untypical of Lewesians. What might have appeared from outside as standard home counties territory has proved in fact to be something of a cockpit of "alternativeness", frequently anti-establishment and often downright weird (see especially "Lewes Bonfire" on the web). I knew we'd feel right at home.

After four or five months Margaret and Mairi began to notice that I hadn't been around much and came south to find me. From my lodgings with Mrs Thompson, we moved into a county council-owned house in an outlier of Brighton called Woodingdean. You can tell just by looking at the relevant Ordnance Survey map that Woodingdean is, well, plain wrong. It just sits there, draped across the contours of the South Downs. What were they thinking of? Sorry, a bit of geography coming though there...

Anyway, I have two recollections of life in Woodingdean. Three if you count Mairi initially refusing to move to Lewes on the grounds that Woodingdean's video rental store had a great plastic gun in its toy box and that the fish and chip takeaway had a life-size model of a fisherman on the roof which was dressed as Santa every Christmas. (And still is).

Where were we? One of Margaret's landmark birthdays arrived a few weeks after we moved to Woodingdean and to celebrate, we decided to spend the Saturday night across the Channel in Dieppe, travelling as foot passengers by ferry from Newhaven. So far, so good. The crossing was blowy but Margaret dosed herself appropriately and it was nothing we couldn't handle. On arrival we had a pleasant afternoon and evening. On the Sunday morning we admired the spectacular waves crashing onto the beach, then enjoyed a pleasant cup of coffee in town before heading to the ferry terminal, which looked suspiciously quiet. We were greeted with the words, "You don't think we sail in THAT, do you?" Actually it was more like "Zut alors! Incroyable!" Something like that. Ah - problem.

We were told that had we turned up earlier, we might have had the benefit of a complimentary coach transfer to Calais, from where ferries were still believed to be sailing. We were however free to take ourselves by train to Calais – via Paris, on a Sunday – but our chances of getting to the ferry terminal in time were, frankly, limited. After some amiable Anglo-French banter about the prospect of better weather on the morrow, we decided to check back into our hotel, where we knew they did at least accept our credit card.

We had one or two tricky practicalities to sort. Firstly, Margaret and I were both due back at work the next day, Monday. This being somewhat before the days of widespread mobile phones and emails, we had to try to make contact with colleagues to alert them. We also had four-year-old Mairi booked to fly as an "unaccompanied minor" to her grandparents in Scotland for the first half term of her primary school career. This meant we had to make contact with Heathrow to change the flight to the Tuesday. (Can you remember having to find a UK phone number when abroad before the days of websites?) This being satisfactorily accomplished, I ran a bath for a relaxing soak, which was when I suddenly remembered we owned two cats, Purdey and Bridget, at home in Woodingdean.

Expecting to be away from Saturday morning to Sunday evening, and having as yet met no neighbours, we had left food out for them – for one night. They were on very unfamiliar, possibly hostile, territory, living in a small house with a solid back yard with high walls and, presumably, no pooing capacity. We had nobody to contact. They would have to deploy their northern grit and fend for themselves.

We found that with no cash, no car and no shops open, an extremely wet and windy Sunday in Dieppe is little different from the way it would have been in Newhaven. It's all fine in December, we discovered, when the shops in Dieppe open on Sunday afternoons for Christmas shopping as well as the hypermarkets, but a rainy late October, no thanks. The cats were perfectly OK when we eventually got home by the way, if you've been worrying.

Two months later, in the run-up to our first and only Woodingdean Christmas, I bought a turkey. Our temporary home had no fridge, no garage and little space but, with two cats on the prowl, we had to hide the bird somewhere until the big day. Stuffing a turkey into the microwave for safe keeping is, we discovered, one of that long list of things you only do once.

Mother-in-law had been down to visit and exchange presents, and I drove her to Euston on Christmas Eve to put her on the train home to Scotland. On the way back to Lewes I stopped for a break at Pease Pottage services at the bottom of the M23 and phoned Margaret to report progress. "Are you near any shops?" was her terse greeting. "The turkey honks. The fowl is, well, foul. You'll need to pick up something else for Christmas dinner".

This at about 7.15 pm on Christmas Eve and I hadn't really got to know the area yet. I headed swiftly to a large supermarket at Brighton marina which had always seemed to be open and found it had closed for Christmas at four. I sped (safely, officer) home to Woodingdean and arrived at 7.55 at the corner store, which was very firmly shut and displayed a notice on the door saying "Closing at 8 on Christmas Eve". (The owner told me a few days later with a chuckle that he'd decided to close early as there were no customers.) So, not even a pack of sausages to decorate with holly.

Margaret was right, the turkey smelt appalling, but I'm from the post-war generation that regards even a mouldy slice of bread as something you are obliged to eat up before you're entitled to any pudding. On Christmas morning I shoved the bird in the oven anyway. Because we were convinced there were things living in the purple shag pile of our council house and we were reluctant to spend more time on it or in it than strictly necessary, we set off into Brighton for a walk round the marina and along the prom to the Palace pier, where we wished that at least one of the fish-and-chip stalls could have been open.

In the event, we ate the damn turkey, spent an anxious afternoon not straying far from the house, and survived. Sad to tell, the microwave didn't. No end of scrubbing or prolonged application of advanced chemical treatments could make an impression on the stench of gamey poultry kept too long in a confined space, and it went to the great microwave recycling centre in the sky. Things, as I say, you only do once.

With the family and cats now in Sussex, Mairi in primary school in Lewes and me working for the County Council, we bought a house of our own on the edge of the county town and moved back to Lewes.

Margaret soon found work as a locum with a number of veterinary practices and I discovered new joys from being the vet's partner. At one all-female surgery the practice Christmas dinner required the presence of the "other halves". I don't know what the vets got out of it but we spare parts, unlikely ever to meet under any other circumstance, were obliged to talk entertainingly to complete strangers. I was told to stay off politics. I don't "do" cars or electronic gizmos, so my opening gambits and witty ripostes were not of an acceptable, workmanlike standard. Football often works well for filling the gaps, but not with everyone. For me, getting irredeemably "over tired" on the house white proved the ideal solution and, with Margaret clearly encountering similar issues at my work "dos", we agreed to be unavailable in future for each other's work-based events.

To be fair, occasional poo amongst the follicles aside, the wife does clean up well of an evening and can often be safely taken out to mix in polite society. She had however grown weary of being introduced as a vet and consequently either upbraided for the astronomic fees they charge ("for doing absolutely nothing"), or drawn into interminable conversation about some lovable pet's unique qualities or near-death experience ("He's still licking his penis, you know. Another orange juice?"), or a daughter's professional ambitions in veterinary nursing. And there are limits to how often you want to be confronted by some overweight idiot dropping his trousers to display his operation scar for comparative purposes. Margaret preferred to claim she was in fact employed as something less socially awkward - a tax inspector, or parking attendant, or part-time pole dancer. Mind you, such an attempt to avoid parrot disease-related dialogue during the evening could prove the source of some unexpectedly tricky conversation if her interlocutor pursued the subject of her "pretend occupation" or showed any personal familiarity with it. "You people have ticketed me six times in Lewes already this year and I swear I've never once been more than two minutes over".

In truth, Margaret's own social skills can be a little

challenging. Woe betide any friend or neighbour sociably informing us of a new canine acquisition. "Oh, *not* a Westie! How expensive is *that* going to be? A collie? Well, as my old uni lecturer used to say, never trust a bull or a collie! Great Dane? They don't live long you know – have you warned your children? A Cavalier? What, r*eally*?"

A mongrel may well prove to be the answer, but that of course depends on the question. There has been a recent trend to breed deliberate crosses, starting with the "Labradoodle" to combine the temperament of a Labrador with whatever a Poodle does – struts round picking up its own hairs or something. But we do now seem to be getting into the area of encouraging liaisons in order to produce memorable names. The vets in my family report a crossing between a Cocker Spaniel and a Poodle to claim a Cockerdoodle and an accidental mating between a Bedlington Terrier and a Springer Spaniel for the product of which the proud owner insisted the vaccine certification should record a Bedspring. We await the arrival of our first cross between a Shih Tzu and just about any breed (Bulldog, perhaps? Jack Russell?)

One veterinary practice Margaret hired herself out to held the contract for supervising greyhound racing at a local track, so she soon took on part of that work and urgently acquired the additional specialist knowledge that was needed. Strict guidelines had to be followed for the transport, preparation and welfare of the dogs on race day. They could be barred from competing if, for example, they had been caught in traffic and spent too long on the road, if they had become dehydrated and lost significant weight through stress, barking and panting in the kennels, or showed signs of carrying an injury or illness when being paraded by the trainers prior to the race. An excited greyhound can make an awful lot of noise, and it made sense to have one's ear plugs handy.

Any suspicion of unauthorised use of drugs in treating the greyhounds or in their feed could of course be dynamite. My brother, years earlier, prescribed for one greyhound bitch small quantities of strychnine to be mixed into her feed as a general pick-me-up. The owner had been using it undiluted, found it spiced up the dog's racing performance no end and was keen to have a repeat prescription.

John had spent an evening himself, as a youngster seeing practice, at a local greyhound track. One of his tasks was to check the identity of each dog against its papers – this was long before micro-chipping. Since betting was a key purpose of the evening, there was an advantage to be gained by switching dogs or tampering with them to beat the form book. Doping could be difficult to detect before the advent of blood testing if administered by an expert, but in unsophisticated hands it could be obvious – if, for example, the dog was so sleepy it could hardly be persuaded to get up, let alone run. One greyhound was presented for veterinary inspection with a noticeably swollen doughy stomach. Since one way of slowing a dog down was to give it a meal of bread and milk shortly before the race, this was something the vet was always on the lookout for. "Either this animal is pregnant or you've just fed it. Since it's got balls it's probably the latter, and in either case it can't run", was the vet's verdict.

Having watched his colleague at work, John was given the task of pretending to be the vet for the last couple of races on the card while the real vet retired to the bar with the veterinary nurses. With all the authority of his student years and a white coat, he thoroughly palpated the dogs, checked them out and was relieved to find no reason to eliminate any of them. He followed his colleague up to the bar. Joining them at the table, he reached for his pint and was disconcerted to realise that his hand was heavily stained with black dye. "They've marked one of the dogs up to match another's identity, the buggers", was the vet's comment. "Not to worry − it just means their 'ringer' managed to get past our 'ringer'!"

Greyhound racing in this country may not take place on quite the scale that it did during the 1950s, and in front of smaller crowds, but there are still a couple of dozen tracks in the United Kingdom and a thriving live audience and betting industry.

The standard format is for six greyhounds to race over varying distances, competing against others similarly graded for ability and "track record". Typically in this country the dogs wear distinctive racing colours, identifying not the owner, as with horses, but the trap the dog is drawn in to start the race − red, blue, white, black, orange and black and white stripes. The dogs race after a "lure" − an artificial, but not particularly lifelike, hare or rabbit − and the call "It's running!" invariably catches the attention of all in the stadium.

Not once, one assumes, has the lure turned out to justify the dogs' efforts in reaching it first but, with greyhounds moving like Exocet missiles round a tight track in a clear case of hope triumphing over experience, and competing for position on the bends, there are inevitably injuries which need to be treated and even the possibility of termination. They are fantastic athletes, with hearts as big as a man's, but occasionally with serious bad breath issues. Not all of them of course necessarily enjoy the racing – they're not asked.

Greyhounds that become too old – or damaged - to race competitively, or have simply failed to perform at the highest level, are not always treated kindly when their track days come to an end. But there is at least one charity in this country (and we're generally better at this than other nations) dedicated to their well-being, the Retired Greyhound Trust, which has an excellent record of finding suitable new homes. Greyhounds generally make great pets and will take as little or as much exercise as they are given. Unfortunately the lure training can mean that they regard cats as a reasonable quarry. Friends of ours took one of these retired racing greyhounds and found him a delightful family pet but were disappointed to discover that the dog had never learned to play, or even to run with other dogs socially. It had become institutionalised through living in race kennels. Though much loved by his post-racing family, Luke remained inhibited and wary and this is, I gather, more or less the norm.

Of course, the official track vet has wide-ranging powers, not confined to the activities or wellbeing of the individual dogs. If the temperature, for example, is near zero and the track appears icy, it will be for the vet to determine whether any racing at all takes place, with all the implications for the track staff, trainers, caterers and the public that entails – and ultimately the financial balance sheet for the evening.

My highlight would have to be the racing Afghans. One evening programme at the Hove track included a charitable fundraiser in the presence of one or two celebrities (we had Noel Edmonds once – how cool is that?) featuring a race between half a dozen long-haired Afghan hounds. Now, whatever other attributes these woolly What-a-Mess lookalikes may possess, naked speed allied to total focus on the job in hand isn't one of them. The one dog that seemed to grasp the concept of the competition and cantered cheerfully round the track was always going to prove the undisputed winner; the other "competitors" were simply too easily distracted – by each other, by the moon perhaps, who knows. Perhaps they have other nights when they race cats. Or squirrels.

I did enjoy my evenings and pie and chips at the racing when Margaret was working and sometimes took friends along with me, as she wasn't in a position to spend much time in the public areas between duties. If she did acquire any useful inside knowledge that might have given me an advantage over the bookies, she was useless at passing it on.

Her attitude to the whole thing was ambivalent. There were clearly plenty of trainers who were excellent and cared for their dogs well. Others didn't gain her respect and gave the impression that their dogs were simply a means of trying to make money. But it was essential that someone with appropriate knowledge and experience was present to look after the animals' welfare.

The greyhound work brought a couple of excellent CPD events. For those who have been spared the term, Continuing Professional Development is a posh way of saying that we should all carry on trying throughout our working lives to get better at doing our jobs. It's all very sensible but can involve a lot of form-filling and box-ticking. Anyway, during her "greyhound years", Margaret signed up for two weekends away, in Birmingham and Dublin. I went with her, not to the workshops, you understand, but to enjoy myself nearby. Our Birmingham trip included a fire alarm at the hotel, triggered by young revellers and resulting in us all being turned out into the streets, not looking our best in "night time apparel" in the early hours, but Dublin was ace as usual and meant I could go and do touristy things on my own, like the Guinness tour and Kilmainham Gaol.

It was around this time that the vet-about-the-house had a very unsatisfactory encounter with one of her least favourite dog breeds. Frankly, one has to wonder about the types who like to walk the streets with untrustworthy dogs. Margaret may feel, for professional reasons, inhibited from being totally honest here. I don't have to. So, you owners of Rottweilers and the like, TOSSERS!

Remember this is a woman who has coped professionally over many years with everything from raging bulls to homicidal boars to a hamster hanging from her fingertip by its teeth, but resented having to defend herself at work with her bare hands against a Rotty with attitude and an inadequate owner. Result: hospitalisation of vet for nearly a week with septicaemia and deep wounds to both arms incurred in protecting her face. Of course we were all relieved it was nothing worse but, come on, this was very inconsiderate on the vet's part, requiring me to become a single parent household while expecting me to carry on doing my own job – and visiting her in hospital!

When recovered, the vet was soon put back to work. For one practice, helping the owner to promote the business and build up trade, she took on an unpaid additional task of writing occasional articles about pets and their care for a local lifestyle magazine. These covered sensitive issues like euthanasia and the need for timely and appropriate vaccinations, and there was one called "Fleas... Let the Battle Commence". Margaret would often put a draft of her article in front of me to see if I, as a layman, could follow it. Always a joy – you're just piling enthusiastically into your fish and chip takeaway when a piece of paper is shoved under your nose reading, and I quote verbatim from the published article, "Fleas can carry tapeworms too. Small, white structures resembling grains of rice in your pet's faeces or on the hair around the anus are tapeworm segments, which means he may also have fleas." "Does that read all right?" she said. "Do you want the vinegar?"

I particularly enjoyed her article, "The Easter Bunny... Make Mine Chocolate", which asked readers to think carefully before buying an adorable, cuddly rabbit as a gift for a child until they had considered practicalities like cost, maintenance and character. This didn't go down at all well with the veterinary practice that Margaret was working for at the time as the owner was concerned that it might discourage people from buying them as pets altogether, with consequential loss of business to the practice. He demanded changes to the text of the article.

Although predominantly a "small animal" (pet) practice, one client was a hobby farmer who, to save expense, preferred to bring his sheep into the surgery for a consultation, vaccination or treatment rather than request a home call. This usually occurred two sheep at a time. Generally the husband or the wife, whoever brought them in, was able to keep the patients firmly under control, but it was not unknown for the sheep to become excited by their surroundings and the proximity of barking dogs, meowing cats and squawking parrots, and set about demolishing the leaflet stands – which did little to calm the other occupants of the waiting room.

There was the occasional equine case which would mean a trip out from the surgery. Not usually a problem. Unless of course you're Margaret, off duty and dressed for an afternoon concert in Brighton with your husband and just happen to drop by the stables which your boss has been called out to so you can get him to sign something. On this particular day, the boss was struggling in a field with a colt castration. He had removed one testicle but found the horse was coming round from the anaesthetic too quickly, before he could finish the job. When Margaret turned up, both he and the veterinary nurse were occupied at the "business end", so to prevent the colt from attempting to rise to its feet she held its head firmly to the very muddy ground, which she found she could achieve only by lying down on top of it. After a few years of being married to a vet I suppose you should get used to arriving late at things like concerts, plays and dinner parties with your partner sporting an intriguing and provocative mud slick across her entire front.

For a while Margaret signed up to work for a Brighton-based vet practice that specialised in providing out-of-hours emergency cover for other surgeries. It's an important part of veterinary work but not one that everybody relishes, hence the extra cash to be earned by those who take it on. This meant my other half setting off to work with her sleeping bag and plenty of reading material at Saturday lunchtime and not coming home until Monday morning, and me doing my single-parent routine for the weekend. I thought of joining a support group.

One urgent case she treated in this capacity was a cat brought in late at night by an agitated father and young daughter and "presenting with" a sudden tumorous growth between the claws of a front paw. Careful examination of the cat was followed by deft use of the vet's fingers and removal of a snail shell. Result: one happy, if slightly embarrassed, and considerably poorer family.

Margaret accepted an invitation to judge the children's pet competition in a local village show. With hindsight, this may have been a mistake. Having in good faith carefully examined all the entrants in every class of bird and animal, she awarded the overall blue riband prize to an excellently turned-out guinea pig – only to be informed by a distinctly put-out villager that the community would have expected something better from their vet than a toadying to the local bigwig, father of the owner of the winning guinea pig. She declined the invitation to repeat the experience at the following year's show.

Despite this faux pas, and in my capacity as a member of the PTA for Mairi's primary school in Lewes, I asked Margaret if she would take on the running of a pet show at school. This proved to be an equally challenging event. Aware that it might prove tricky to judge, say, a cat against a goldfish, it seemed a good idea to ask the children about their pets and how they looked after them as a basis for ranking. I stood deferentially behind the vet with my clipboard as Margaret interviewed one child after another. To be frank here, at least one of the little creatures was alive with fleas. And that went for the pets too.

"What do you feed the cat/dog/goldfish on?" she would ask.

This would routinely be answered with silence and a shyly questioning glance at a handily placed parent.

"You know. That's the cat food/dog food/fish food you give him twice a day."

The alleged pet-loving child would repeat the answer to the vet, sometimes correctly.

"And how often do you clean him out?"

Again, the shy glance.

"That would be once a week".

And again the conscientious and pet-adoring child would pass on the answer.

At that age, you probably have to worry more about the parents accepting the outcome of the competition than the kids themselves. Somehow the school's own terrapins emerged as a reasonably safe winner.

Enthused by the roaring success of this initiative, the school's reception class teacher suggested to Margaret that it would be fun to set up a vet's surgery in the classroom and could she bring in a few tricks of the trade to show her little charges? The vet duly obliged and took along some bandages, a stethoscope and an array of scary-looking instruments for the children to handle, which were then applied randomly to assorted teddy bears and other favourite cuddlies. She also displayed an X-ray depicting a fracture as obvious as the Great East African Rift Valley. A great time was had by all. As Margaret explained, "If it prevents just one youngster from spending his or her formative years training to be a vet when they could be out on the streets having a good time, then my visit will not have been wasted. Sorry, joking!"

During the school holidays it usually fell to one of the teachers to take any classroom pets home with them, but Mairi decided one term to offer her mum's services in this respect and turned up at home with two large rats. Unfortunately Margaret couldn't fail to spot that one was carrying a very large, ulcerated, mammary tumour and was almost certainly suffering with it. Having contacted Mairi's class teacher, she did the only professional thing she could do. Which meant that, from then on, she was referred to by Mairi's classmates as the lady that killed our school pet. (My brother once received several repeat visits from a family with rats bearing a succession of mammary tumours but that turned out to be because the father, who worked at a medical research laboratory, had been stealing them from work).

John tells me the question he is most frequently asked after giving a talk, especially to children, is to identify the smallest and the biggest creatures he has dealt with over his years as "Northumberland's longest serving vet". He cites freeze-dried ragworm, almost invisible to the naked eye, as the smallest, having been asked to certify a consignment of them as fit for use as fishing bait or as a feedstuff on a fish farm. The largest was an emaciated young female sei whale, eight metres long – though they run to more than twice that length - lying distressed on a Northumbrian beach, which he was called out to terminate.

My nephew Sam, by now a partner in the same Northumberland practice as his father, had a rewarding experience addressing a local primary school. Having delivered his carefully-prepared talk and shown a few small mammals, he invited questions. The first hand was raised.

"You treated our hamster last year when it was sick."

"Ah yes. And how is it?"

"It died."

A second hand went up.

"One of your lady vets came to our house last week to see our dog."

"And?"

"She killed it. She said she had to."

Sam decided not to risk any more audience participation, accepted the round of handclapping ordered by the form teacher and slipped quietly away.

CHAPTER SEVEN

REIGNING CATS AND DOGS, AND PONIES

"My lovely horse running through the field,
Where are you going with your fetlocks blowing in the wind?
Running around with a man on your back like a train
in the night, like a train in the night."

G. Linehan, A. Mathews, N. Hannon My Lovely Horse,
A Song for Europe (Father Ted)

"I don't know why I'm bothering to teach you about the horse's
brain – all you really need to know is where to put the bullet"

Veterinary medicine lecture, 1980

At home we acquired an increasing number of pets as Mairi grew old enough to demand them. Purdey and Bridget, the Mancunian cats we had brought south with us, were soon supplemented by Peanuts, a locally-sourced ginger tom kitten. The older cats had never accepted that Mairi was here to stay, so we encouraged Peanuts to chum up with the daughter by plonking him into her bed for the first night or two, and it worked. This being our first male cat, I hadn't previously experienced the sight of Margaret whipping off the male naughty bits and it did cause my eyes to water a fraction – that and the thinly-veiled caution that began with the words "Of course, if I ever caught you up to no good..."

Nineteen years later as I write this, Peanuts is still with us – though, as Margaret eventually had to terminate the other two at that age, he shouldn't bank on being around much beyond that. We've been sent numerous links over recent years to websites featuring dozens of cats from all around the globe undertaking hilarious activities with computer printers or simply looking at the camera in a funny way but Peanuts has, let's be honest, been a bit of a disappointment to us in this respect. Margaret says he's a very loving cat and, to be fair, he does take up some interesting positions when trying to lick his non-existent extremities – the one where he gets his leg up behind his ear is, frankly, impressive – but he's never come near to building a successful internet career. Perhaps this is something that ambitious cat owners might be able to breed for in the future.

We went through some of the common children's pets, like hamsters, guinea pigs and gerbils, with Mairi (like many other children, she would wish me to stress) frequently starting off over-enthusiastically but gradually losing interest and leaving the chores to her parents. I'm afraid Margaret and I did once give away two guinea pigs plus cage to another family in Lewes without asking Mairi, as we felt they needed more attention than they were getting, or were likely to get, and she would always promise to devote more time to them without putting it into practice. A couple of weeks later Mairi went into the conservatory where the guinea pigs had been kept and asked where they were. There was, naturally, pandemonium when she was told the awful truth, but it was hard to sustain a legitimate grievance once she was told how long it had taken her to miss them.

The mortality of pets is an issue for children – and for the rest of us, of course. Mairi had her two gerbils (brothers) out on the bedroom floor one day while there were friends round to play. The noise and frenzied activity obviously proved too much for the furry rodents and the children suddenly discovered that the gerbils had clashed in the middle of the floor and fought and one had, in fact, killed its brother. This was traumatic at a number of levels and we decided the next day to recognise the creature's passing with a small, "close family only" ceremony in the back garden. We were moved to see that Mairi had put together a small stick-based cross bearing the words, "You were a true and loyal jerble".

Goldfish can also of course be sods for dying on you. We bought two fish to put in a tank in the kitchen and after much family discussion named them, but a week or two later found them floating upside down. We repeated the process until we started to run out of names and it was all proving very depressing, not least for the fish. Meanwhile, in our garden pond, fish seemed to appear from nowhere and thrive. So, after four or five disasters with our indoor acquisitions, Mairi suggested we net a few of the clearly hardy specimens from outside and try them in the house. We also resolved that under no circumstances would we ever give them names. SUCCESS! Our four relocated fish lived happily (as far as we could tell they showed no signs of being stressed by whatever news or weather reports they were picking up from the TV in the corner of the room) for nearly ten years. Until, that is, the introduction of either new live plants or water fleas from the pet shop appears to have introduced disease to the unsuspecting and unprotected population. I won't seek to equate this process with what happened to the Incas but the outcome was comparable in percentage terms. Two of the four died immediately and the others acquired an unusual line in colouring and adopted unprecedented patterns of movement. We got ourselves down to the pet shop forthwith, not to litigate for the dodgy water fleas but to buy a new, and much bigger, tank. Ignoring the usual protocol of balancing the chemical make-up and temperature of the water in the new tank with the old, we simply netted the two survivors and chucked them into the fresh water. We're another ten years down the line and, touch wood, they're still with us. And they're of a size where Peanuts the cat wouldn't want to mess with them if they got out for a wander round.

The garden pond has over the years been the source of much entertainment. Birds splash in the kind of fountain thing; dragonflies and damselflies course over the surface. Fish arrive and depart, we know not where, although we have spotted the occasional heron. We have seen frogs, toads and newts spawning and growing there in considerable numbers but, apart from the depredations of the goldfish, we have never quite worked out what causes their numbers to wax and wane. We have annually witnessed what we used to call "frog cuddling day" in the spring when the pond became a seething Sodom and Gomorrah of carnal activity and you wouldn't want to put your toes in. This is now generally referred to in the household as "frog bonking day", but then, Mairi is some twenty years older.

This was also about the time when Mairi, like many girls of her age, got heavily into ponies. This was always going to be a possibility, what with Margaret having done plenty of riding of her own, so I was outnumbered from the start. Would they listen to me? Ha! "This," I declared firmly to the awaiting family, "is going to cost us. Big time." But, did they take any notice? Margaret pointed out that vets' bills amounted to a significant part of the expense and those costs could largely be discounted.

In the event her familiarity with the construction and layout details of the equine species proved to be a tad less fresh than anticipated and Margaret decided that the old vet college books would need to be revisited. Or, to be specific, that it was *my* job to find her old text books in the loft.

"That's your domain dear, the loft. It can't be that difficult. I mean, what else is there up there? The Christmas tree stand, that ridiculous old tent you refuse to part with and your Pentangle LPs? Incidentally, why don't you just get rid of all those LPs? There must be hundreds of them and it's not as if you're ever going to be playing them again. At least, not while I'm alive. And certainly not that Barclay James whoever."

"Harvest. Barclay James Harvest. Loads of dry ice. You do remember what happened the last time I went up there?"

"I'm sure you're going to remind me."

"We were trying to find where the wasps on the landing were coming from. I moved that enormous straw coloured thing in the loft out of the way to look behind it. When I picked it up, I realised where they were coming from. I didn't know wasps did honeycombs. But I do now. You'll miss me when I've gone, you know. You'll have to do your own loft sorties."

"It's very simple. You do manly things in the loft and put the recycling boxes down the drive; I set timers when we go on holiday and shout at the broadband helpline man. We're a team."

Mm.

I'm not sure lofts have been re-evaluated recently in the same way that sheds have. I don't mean loft conversions; I'm talking about overstuffed junk yards in the sky. A chap could contentedly pass a month or two up there rediscovering his certificate for coming second in the potato race at prep school or his prize compilation book of poetry, never opened, for good attendance at cubs.

Anyway, the battered vet books eventually came to light and Margaret spent several evenings poring over them, becoming increasingly convinced that somehow the equine anatomical arrangements had changed since her day.

"Ok, then", I said, retreating to a pre-prepared second line of defence, "just a few riding lessons and borrowing other children's ponies, until she gets bored like with the guinea pigs, or discovers boys."

In the event we copped for the lot. First there were the lessons at the local riding school, usually on a Saturday morning. I developed a technique I thought was pretty neat, giving the impression I was watching while reading the newspaper below the parapet, timing my look up and wave at just the right moment to appear thoroughly engaged. Then there was all the expensive kit. Boy, there was the kit.

And then, horror of horrors, we somehow moved onto needing access to our own steed. I'm delighted to say that we managed to avoid ever actually owning the freehold on one but we did take out a succession of full repairing leases on ponies that belonged to friends, or friends of friends. That meant paying for the stabling but enjoying the benefit of being able to do our own mucking out. This time I did dig in; I paid the bills but drew the line at doing any work. This, I'm pleased to say, fell to Mairi's mother, which was only as it should be.

The three of us would share the trip to the stable (actually various stables in different locations on the South Downs around Lewes, depending on the pony) with Mairi riding, Margaret shovelling horse poo and me walking the dog, of which more anon. Provided my position of non-combatant remained inviolate I was content. There were worse places to be on a summer evening than out with the Labrador on the chalk escarpment.

The pony phase actually lasted quite a long time and included, as I recall, at least one gymkhana competing against assorted youngsters and their scary mothers who reminded me unnervingly of the subjects of old Thelwell cartoons. Was I really part of this, or could I maintain a kind of ironic disengagement? My own riding efforts had been confined to perching on top of some safely aged riding school hack like a sack of spuds when on holiday in the Rockies or some other memorable landscape to make up the numbers.

I had joined Margaret and a few of her colleagues back in the pre-Mairi days on a pony-trekking weekend in north Wales and had ended up losing my stirrups, sliding precariously to one side as the pony headed off on a journey of its own choosing. I hung on to its neck from a sideways-on position and suddenly experienced a flashback to an old TV western series called, if memory serves, Range Rider – theme tune "Home, home on the range where the deer and the antelope play". Can that be right? Antelope? Anyway, the opening credits featured (how is it that I can remember this stuff when I can't remember why I just went to open a kitchen cupboard?) someone or other playing the part of Dick West, All American Boy and he was, thrillingly, firing his Colt 45 *underneath* his horse's neck at some unspecified foe. Magic - though I suspect with the benefit of several decades of hindsight that the target may have been a number of more poorly-armed indigenous Americans and therefore his actions may have been at best questionable in ethical and racial terms. That, at any rate, was the heroic self-image I contrived to capture in the split second before the bl**dy thing dumped me in the gorse.

My wife and daughter are both made of sterner, or more

pliable, stuff and would go on quite long rides along the downs. Margaret would borrow an eleven-year-old retired racehorse called Robert, who was essentially bonkers but safe. He always seemed very interested in the world about him and would follow Margaret round the paddock as she picked up his poo, clearly impressed that anyone should think it worth retaining. For some unfathomable reason he would become terribly distracted and upset by any itinerant crisp packet and one would often hear the warning call from wife to daughter, or vice versa, "Plastic bag alert!"

Around this time my work at County Hall included responsibility for road safety in the county and the idea of roadside "shrines" was catching on. Bereaved relatives of people killed in traffic accidents had taken to laying flowers and other more personal objects at the scene and, while this seemed a perfectly reasonable form of commemoration for those most affected, others were beginning to object. Elderly people living in houses nearby complained that they didn't wish to have an informal but persistent memorial facing them, and presumably reminding them of their own mortality, whenever they set foot outside. But the most strongly written letters of objection were coming from horse riders whose mounts were distracted by spinning windmills and, yes, the dreaded fluttering of plastic bags, and said these were a source of some hazard.

The sudden appearance in the sky one summer evening, as we walked and rode together along the chalk ridge, of a couple of hang gliders brought a whole extra dimension to the concept of "hazard", and Mairi's shout of "Mum, Robert's nostrils have gone square!" was the prelude to Robert and his rider disappearing into the distance at near racing speed until they became a small dot. It was a good half hour later when the two, fortunately still attached, returned, white-faced, legs trembling (Margaret) and looking sheepish (Robert).

Sadly, Robert didn't get to spend a long and contented retirement, troubled only by the confectionary products of Walkers and Pringle. Margaret, in full professional mode, became aware of the development of a major breathing problem in him and called in a specialist equine vet who found he was in effect breathing with only one lung. Although only eleven, there was no alternative to euthanasia and it was a sad time for us all.

One of the other owners using the same stables used to bring her Jack Russell with her to "help". Like all of his breed, he suffered from "Seabiscuit Syndrome", being convinced he was bigger than he was. He would weave in and out between the horses' hooves, yapping a challenge to them to "bring it on". One evening he was hurtling after a rabbit when he ploughed into a barbed wire fence. When he returned to face us, demanding action on the ball or stick front, he had taken on a kind of jaunty French Foreign Legion look, with almost the whole of the skin from the top of his head hanging in a loose flap, exposing a glistening mass of red muscle. This seemed, even to me, to merit prompt remedial action and Margaret went to open up her surgery in order to staple the natty new headgear back into place. Somehow one felt that, this being merely a "flesh wound" to the Jack Russell, he would happily have foregone the general anaesthetic in order to retain his image of "hard".

This working with horses business isn't always all it's cracked up to be. Ask Margaret. She drove to the stables before dawn one morning to muck out and prepare feed before going to work at her proper job. She carried out her duties by the light of the car headlamps. Regrettably, this meant the car wouldn't start when she'd finished. I was still asleep at home and she had to run the three miles back to Lewes in the dark along a winding road with no pavement and a gradually building early morning rush hour.

Nor, despite my most determined efforts, was I allowed to remain completely exempt from these chores – as if I needed reminding of how questionable this whole horsey thing was.

I took a call from Margaret, claiming she was delayed by an emergency at work and could I possibly step in like a true hero and "do the horses". Funny how this only seemed to happen on dark, wet days. Anyway, I went straight to the stables from County Hall in my suit of bureaucrat grey and my mincing about the office shoes and soon detected what could only be described as a complete absence of wellies, hats or waterproofs. Great. Robert and Mischief stood looking as miserable as I felt at the gate to their field and the rain was now "sheeting" down (this is a family book). I paddled out into the mud and managed to lead them in one at a time. I'd seen it done but not really observed the details before and it wasn't easy keeping one back in the field while extricating the first. I worked out that the soaking blankets they had worn in the field might not be the best thing for them to spend the night in. (I liked my family to know that I wasn't up for all this stuff, but some of it kind of rubbed off despite everything). I wasn't sure whether horses were self-drying but I gave them a bit of a wipe anyway, then made up something that looked vaguely like a bed and an evening meal. But were they likely to fancy a spot of supper as well later on?

At last I decided I was done, checked that I hadn't left anything looking too barmy, and took my incipient pneumonia home with me. Margaret, true to form, went up to the stables anyway once she'd reached home in order to check my handiwork. Bless.

On another occasion when our shared pony was stabled at the grandstand of the old Lewes racecourse, Margaret had gone up there on foot in thick fog with just the dog for company. When she had completed her tasks, she went outside and found the thick swirling greyness utterly disorientating and couldn't find the dog anywhere, despite wandering vaguely around for half an hour shouting for her. Eventually Margaret managed to find her own way home through the fog, hoping to enlist support in a search, but found Molly dog sitting on the front step waiting for her.

Molly was a treasure. One of the few family pets we actually paid money for, she was something of a runt in a pedigree litter of black Labradors from West Sussex, with a flatter head and leaner physique than might be regarded as ideal by the purists.

But as a family pet she couldn't be bettered. She filled Mairi's desire for a friend who was always totally available and dependable and could safely be shown off to schoolmates and their parents. We took her to a course of obedience classes, or whatever they call them, in Lewes with Mairi in pole position at the other end of the lead and us parents watching helplessly from the sidelines. Being extremely biddable by nature, I suppose Molly was unlikely actually to fail her exam but, after decades of feeling tested at school (this is me now, not Molly), university and throughout my career, I still felt butterflies in my stomach as I waited anxiously for the affirmation of success. I think that makes me officially a sad person.

Molly knew her place in the hierarchy, which was some way below the two older cats. It was an easy source of cheap laughs to roll a favourite ball close to a dozing Purdey, then encourage Molly to fetch; the ensuing unreleased tension could last forever. And one would often find Molly cut off at the wrong end of the upstairs landing by Bridget, sleeping, totally unaware, outside the airing cupboard. The younger Peanuts, however, was made of more conciliatory stuff. He tolerated with good grace being rolled over by an over-enthusiastic pup and eventually came to regard Molly as his best, and possibly only, friend, frequently giving her a sound licking if he found her in the lounge on his return from catting duties elsewhere.

Throughout her life Molly did have a tendency, if she could get away with it, to take herself off round our housing estate to check out anyone who might want to be friends or have food to share. She seemed to have a friendly tail wag for everyone, with just two exceptions, for whom she reserved a low growl – men in baseball caps (which makes perfect sense to me) and, to our embarrassment, anyone of oriental extraction. Goodness knows where that came from, but it never looked good.

We had her phone number (actually it was our phone number) etched into a key tag on her collar and we had her micro-chipped. This is a more or less theft-proof method of marking one's pet as, without going to a vet, it's pretty hard to remove the identification. One day when she was less than a year old she managed to escape from the garden and I wandered round the local streets and countryside calling for her. Returning towards the house from one fruitless circuit I spotted the young son of our close friends and neighbours across the road and asked him if by any chance he had seen Molly in the last hour or so. He said not, but after some thought he added that they had found a black dog in their back garden and were holding onto it to see if the owner appeared. "Are you sure it's not Molly?" I persisted, seriously doubting the coincidence. "No, it's not. Mum said it had a different name on its collar". I thought it worth checking this out and went back to his house with him. Molly greeted me in that enthusiastic but slightly embarrassed way they do in such circumstances. "What's this about some other dog's name then?" I said to Marie Christine, at which she drew my attention to the very clear nomenclature on the collar that read "Scan my Chip". It occurs to me, thinking back to previous comments, that this could have made a fabulous stripper name.

Molly was an excellent surgery dog, going into work with

Margaret each day and settling quietly into any large cage not occupied by dogs awaiting treatment or recovering from it. If no cage was available she could normally be relied on to settle invisibly behind the reception desk, minding her own business and only reappearing, as if my magic, at the end of the day once the clients – and their owners - had all been and gone.

In truth, she was in her element wherever she was taken and always enjoyed mooching around the stables when we were up there. Unfortunately, most dogs seem to find a horse's foot trimmings extremely tasty and Molly, being a Labrador by both breed and nature, was no exception. The day the farrier came to do his work was clearly a highlight in the gastronomic calendar and, however much one tried to keep an eye on her, Molly would somehow manage to dine out on these toothsome morsels. Result: vomit of a particularly unpleasant kind in the kitchen once we got her home.

I'm not sure how it worked out like this but Margaret and I somehow evolved an agreement that, if it was still alive and inside the house (like a fluttery sparrow, for example, or a frog brought in by one of the cats), it was her job, but if it wasn't still alive, or had never officially been alive, like poo or vomit, it was mine. Is that fair? Would it stand up in court if legally challenged? Margaret claimed that nurses do that stuff at the workplace so she didn't have to. What I will say is this: clearing up vomited equine hoof trimmings is bad but, if you really want to see – and smell – something nasty, just try coming down to the kitchen in the morning after your dog has consumed a whole tub of yellow Flora during the night.

Sorry, I've just been taking a moment out to get over that memory and the associated gagging reflex. So, I guess I'm not going to be invited to help advertise that particular product as a potential dog treat anytime soon.

Mairi's interest in pets was never going to run to following in Margaret's blood and mud-spattered veterinary footsteps. Indeed we hoped to discourage her from developing any kind of social or environmental conscience, such as had troubled her parents. This was not entirely successful. She announced one day her plan to set up a stall in the Paddock, a popular green space in the centre of Lewes behind the Norman castle, where she would sell off any toys or games she had grown out of in order to raise funds to "Save the Manatee" – a species not known to be widespread in Sussex waters but one she had very much fallen for on a holiday in Florida. This was clearly one of those ideas that sounded just great until you actually thought about it. I couldn't see how we could expose our ten-year-old to the likely disappointment of sitting in the park all day being ignored. But she didn't look likely to fall for the traditional parental technique of diverting her into some other activity until the moment passed. Eventually we came up between us with the plan of hosting her original scheme in our garden and inviting our, and her, own guests. In addition to Mairi's "bedroom toy sale" and a number of entrance fee-paying games like lucky dip, the event would also feature a "bring and buy" cake baking element.

Fortunately, Save the Manatee day was blessed with wonderful summer weather and our friends and neighbours not only turned up in numbers, bringing their own cake creations, but they spent hours sunbathing and chatting and buying back their own produce to eat, washed down with the most expensive cups of tea in Lewes – well, it was a sellers' market. The money fairly rolled in. Come the end of the afternoon and few of our guests seemed over keen to go home, so out came the family barbecue. Our only problem was that we had little to hand by way of actual meat. Charcoal, yes. Ketchup, yes. Meat, no. So we asked our nearest neighbours if they could help us out and they responded rapidly to the challenge by raiding their fridges. Half an hour later we were able to charge them £2 for their own delicious hot dog or burger. One or two thought it cheeky; I call it "added value".

It was not just manatees. We adopted countless ducks at wildfowl and wetland centres, shire horses and even a couple of white rhinos in Africa which rarely communicated with their adoptive parents and with which we had precious little prospect of bonding.

Closer to home Mairi did get a huge kick out of joining the Junior Advisory Board for a small local zoo called Drusilla's. This has been something of an institution on the South Downs west of Eastbourne for nearly a century, founded by the Ann family as a tea room destination for coach parties, enhanced by aviaries, floral displays, boat rides and other activities. Drusilla had been the first wife of the founder, Douglas Ann, and the place had continued to evolve and thrive ever since.

In the 1990s I knew the then owners, Michael and Kitty

Ann, and had worked with them and others to create a global conference on the environment for around 800 children aged ten to twelve. It was held in Eastbourne, was a remarkable success and one of the most thoroughly enjoyable work experiences I shall ever have. And all initially the idea of the Drusilla's Junior Board set up by Michael and Kitty to advise them, as core customers, on the running of the zoo.

"Zoo" doesn't adequately describe Drusilla's. Perhaps a zoo for people who don't like zoos, with its emphasis on smaller creatures – like meerkats, before they got their own agents - in a decent amount of space, well supported by informative and entertaining displays, and with a strong emphasis on environmental issues and play. Mairi put her name forward and was appointed to the Board, where she served for two years and proudly got to keep her official Board uniform, which comprised a sweatshirt with a tie sort of built into it.

Talking about Drusilla's is reminding me of another animal place, in the Netherlands, that I'm rather more embarrassed about.

The Ankers family always did pretty good holidays, and we aimed to pack variety and interest as well as fun into our trips wherever we went. Mairi might contest this overall claim and has been known to call in evidence our Holiday of Death in the north east of the USA. Personally I thought it was really interesting as well as educational to visit the Arlington cemetery with the Kennedy memorials, Ford's theatre in Washington where Abraham Lincoln was shot, the Peterson house across the street where he died, the Iwo Jima monument, the Vietnam War memorial wall, the Washington monument, the Lincoln memorial... Anyway, I digress. We were cycling in the Netherlands on one of those holidays where they take your bags to the next hotel for you. I had picked up a leaflet - in Dutch - depicting what was clearly a monkey sanctuary with the title 'Oog in Oog' in Appeldoorn. We reached the town of Appeldoorn but could find no sign of the sanctuary. It therefore seemed logical to me to ask passers-by where Oog in Oog might be, but I didn't seem to be getting anywhere. Eventually I think we just happened to pass by on the right road so we got to see the lovable little chaps and have our sunglasses and cameras lifted by them. And at some stage during the visit it belatedly occurred to me that the Oog in Oog to which I had been seeking directions was almost certainly the equivalent of a football fan making apparently racially motivated "monkey gestures".

There's worse.

Another family holiday took us to Corsica, driving there and back through France. We came off the motorway to have lunch in Troyes, then continued for a while on the non-motorway road through the mountains. All very pleasant until we suddenly caught the briefest glimpse of a bird approaching from the side, then felt an impact that made us jump. I glanced in the rear mirror but could see nothing on the road. After about half an hour we drove through a small town. Mairi thought she had seen people looking and pointing at us but I told her she had imagined it. We passed a large shop window, tried to see our reflection and definitely felt that something didn't look quite right. We agreed to carry on to a quieter part of town before stopping to investigate. I pulled in, checked the roof rack and found myself looking straight into the slowly blinking eye of an eagle, or certainly a very sizeable bird of prey with major wingspan issues, trapped under the rack.

I thought it would be helpful to share this new information with Margaret, who hadn't left her seat in the car.

"Is it alive?" she asked.

"Oh yes".

"Well, you obviously can't leave it there. You'll need to get it out and we'll have to take it to someone who can deal with it."

"Are you insane? Have you seen it? This is not something you can pop in a tupperware box for God's sake! It's nearly my size. I'm not touching the bloody thing."

Vets, honestly.

It seemed to me on brief reflection that our best bet might be to get right out of town where we wouldn't be the centre of attention, then either hope to remove the rack without being savaged or prize the bird out using some handy branch. I got back in the driver's seat and set off again. Only a minute or two later, while still driving through town, we felt and heard an enormous crash as the bird hit Mairi's side window. Mairi screamed and I saw the surprised raptor lurching about on the highway in haphazard fashion in the rear view mirror. I stopped the car again.

"What are you going to do now?" enquired Margaret, ever helpful.

"You're the vet. What would you like me to do?"

"Well, you can't just leave it there in the middle of the road".

"I suppose I could drive back there and run over it a few times if you think that would help, but it looks like there are locals starting to gather round to help. On balance I think I'm just going to run away."

Vets and holidays eh? Then there was our trip to Italy, just a week after Mairi had managed to slice her foot open when playing in a friend's garden. Margaret assured the nurse at the local cottage hospital that she was perfectly capable of taking the stitches out when necessary and would take her scary set of curved scalpels with her to Italy for that purpose. When it came time to do the deed in our hotel in Lucca, Margaret looked for the blades in her suitcase. Then she asked me to search in mine. They were eventually located in her handbag.

"Just as a matter of interest, when did you take them out of your case and put them in there?"

"What? Does it matter?"

"Only, I mean, have they been in there all along? As in, did you have them in your handbag when you went through the security scan at the airport?"

"Ah."

So, not as dangerous as a bottle of Coke or shampoo then.

I mentioned a cycling holiday. All three of us have bikes and have been known to use them. We are fortunate to have direct access to the downs behind the house with their extensive network of bridle paths, and a favourite trip involved taking the bikes, and Molly the fit young Labrador, by car to Ditchling Beacon, then cycling home downhill with Molly running alongside – with rests of course.

As both Mairi and I had a daily commute within Lewes, the idea of cycling to school and the office was a real option and I devised a convoluted route to Mairi's primary school taking in some quiet residential roads, a byelaw-infringing route across a park and a couple of extremely hairy road crossings. But it did enable both of us to feel grown up, and guaranteed that we started our working day sweaty.

I marked turning 50 by tackling the annual London to Brighton bike ride with friends, even if I did succumb to a large number of dismounts and bike pushes and managed to snap the chain in the process. I had mixed feelings on returning home with a tender rear end to see a sheet hanging on our garage which proclaimed in purple paint, "Congratulations Baboon Bott".

I also successfully applied for a Churchill Fellowship, which enabled me to spend a month in Denmark and the Netherlands investigating how they went about planning, funding, building and managing their networks of cycle routes. This wasn't merely out of curiosity or just to have a good time – though I did. Having been through a major reorganisation at work I had acquired responsibility for a whole heap of stuff that I knew next to nothing about, the way you do. In my case this meant that I added the minor matter of economic development, transport planning and road safety to my bedrock of environmental work and can but hope that none of you noticed. But I did try to work my green credentials into this wider portfolio, and the promotion of cycling was just one part of this.

Mairi's place of work also changed around this time, as she progressed from her Lewes primary school to a secondary school in nearby Burgess Hill. I never let an absence of male offspring get in the way and could regularly be heard demanding that my daughter "get stuck in" on the netball court – it being officially a non-contact sport. The fact that I knew less than nothing about the rules deterred neither Mairi nor me. She made the Sussex county team for her age group for several years and I loved it, travelling all over the place in support to share my totally uninformed enthusiasm – that is, you know, when we weren't looking round really interesting cemeteries.

Margaret, on the other hand, was roped in by the school to engage in something she did know about, vetting. She hosted visits to her surgery by Duke of Edinburgh Award students and provided them with the required assessment. One girl in particular showed genuine commitment and continued to attend Margaret's workplace to observe her at work as she developed her interest in following a career in veterinary medicine. It has been a source of pleasure and satisfaction that this young lady has continued to update Margaret on her progress.

As Mairi headed towards the sixth form she applied for a scholarship to assist with the fees and we anxiously awaited the crucial call from the school. So, hearing the phone ring in the kitchen and Margaret picking up, Mairi and I headed in that direction, arriving just in time to hear Margaret utter the words down the line, "Exactly which bit of 'insufferable idiot' didn't you understand then?" Then turning towards us, "What? It's OK, it wasn't school. Just my boss."

We knew then that Mum had definitely decided to change jobs.

CHAPTER EIGHT

A LITTLE OLDER,
A LITTLE SILLIER

"If you try to take a cat apart to see how it works, the first thing you have on your hands is a non-working cat."

Douglas Adams, 1952 - 2001

"When you're treating dysentery, watch you don't fall between two stools"

Veterinary medicine lecture, 1979

At the end of 2003 I found that a routine walk uphill with Molly led to a strange iron-like grip being exerted on my chest. I now know this is what they call chest pain and it's a common sign that all is not well with the heart, but I didn't know that at the time. I thought I had a bad case of heartburn or indigestion and tried to walk it off. It took a couple of recurrences before I got round to seeing the GP, who referred me to the Royal Sussex County Hospital in Brighton.

I soon learned that I had a 95% arterial blockage in the worst possible place and was, in their words, a death waiting to happen. Thanks very much, Mum, for the genes and those great cooked breakfasts. They told me to stop work immediately, sit still and wait to be called in for triple bypass surgery.

Though I was told I was highest priority in clinical terms, it nevertheless took a further three months before I was admitted. One's natural stiff upper lip inclination is to assume that others may be worse off and that one should just wait one's turn. With a few weeks still to go I was invited to the hospital for the day, along with other imminent cardiac admissions, in order to see the facilities, meet some of the staff and talk to one or two bypass survivors. It proved an interesting day, not least when we were taken up a steep iron outside stairway to the canteen for lunch. At least, all the others were; I knew very well that the prospect of me getting up those stairs was non-existent as I couldn't cross a room without sitting down to recuperate half way across. They brought a sandwich down to me. At the end of the afternoon, when we were asked if we had any questions, I was impressed to hear more than one query about whether it was a good idea to carry on playing tennis or golf or whatever while awaiting admission for surgery. From that day on I felt no guilt whatsoever in pursuing the admissions guy, enquiring each day about my place on the list.

The bypass operation went well, as far as I could tell at the time, though I did need further surgery two months later after repeated bouts of acute discomfort and nausea and after I was taken in to see the consultant in a wheelchair, having keeled over in the hospital car park.

Strangely, one consideration in my mind as I recovered in hospital after the first operation and was looking forward to getting home, was just how I was supposed to navigate a way into the house past a besotted Labrador. Molly, you will appreciate, was first and foremost *my* dog – at least, that was clearly how she saw it. She was inclined to go over the top if I was out of sight for a few minutes at the shops, so it was difficult to see her taking a relaxed stance on my return to the fold after a full week. I had been given strict instructions about not jeopardising my new internal wiring layout and I'd been told to clutch a pillow to my chest on the drive home from hospital and on all car journeys for the next week or two.

On arrival chez Ankers, Mairi was detailed to hold the dog on the tightest of tight leads at the front door while Margaret helped me up the steps outside, then along the hall to an armchair in the lounge. Molly was then allowed, under strictest supervision and the threat of throttling, to express her greetings. Clearly unimpressed with this arrangement, she succeeded over the next hour in inching her way below the armrest of the chair to a position where her head and increasingly heavy shoulders came to rest on my lap and chest while I formed an entirely captive audience.

After my second operation I still didn't prosper, and over the next few months I had six further readmissions to A and E at the Royal Sussex, sometimes in the middle of the night, when my heart went wildly out of rhythm and I had to be treated with drugs to stabilise the pattern of heartbeats. At one point Margaret put me in front of her laptop to listen via a veterinary website to the heartbeat of a very sick dog with what she said was a similar arrhythmic pattern to my own. I wasn't impressed. She also had a tendency to want to explain to me just what was going on inside my anatomy and what could conceivably have gone wrong at the bypass stage if I'd been unlucky. I have always taken the view that what lurks beneath the bonnet of our car should remain a secret best left to those inducted into its eternal mysteries: I take a similar view with my own internal arrangements.

For more than a month that summer, after two major operations on my heart, numerous readmissions and more or less weekly outpatient appointments, I found I couldn't actually breathe when lying down, so I was spending most of the day and all of the night sitting in the same armchair and not doing very much. You tend to wonder later on why you didn't use all those months off work more productively by learning to speak colloquial Swahili, for example, or how to play the saxophone, but somehow at the time your heart just isn't in it, as it were. I think the limit of my ambition was rearranging my sock drawer and a cursory effort at putting the CDs in alphabetical order. I'm not sure there's really an alternative, but it does require an element of resilience to keep battling on in such circumstances, hoping for the best. That, and a huge amount of support from one's family.

The in-house vet of course could tell that my coat was no longer glossy and wondered if my lack of a cold, wet nose meant

I was suffering from distemper. Fortunately she had the skills to monitor my pulse and recognise a dodgy one when she felt it. She had to cope with driving me at any time of day or night to the hospital, while still turning in a performance at work the next day. We also have some marvellous friends and neighbours who knew how to show support, and I will never underestimate the impact of dozens and dozens of get well cards and messages that continued to arrive from all over. I particularly liked the one I received from a colleague that read on the outside, "Hundreds of people are hoping your operation is an immediate success". Inside it continued, "They're waiting for the bed."

After a while my nights in the armchair came to feel like normality and I certainly caught up on a lot of reading. I am however still scarred by the memory of having decided one night in the wee small hours that I had one too many cushions behind me and so dropped one down beside the chair, straight onto a sleeping but unseen Molly apparently, as her subsequent scream of horror awakened the household. Goodness only knows just how this perceived assault was integrated into her dream, but its impact set my recovery back by weeks.

A chap's dog is of course his constant and reassuring companion through bad times as well as good, and I measured my progress towards full recovery by the walks I was able to take with her. My first official outdoor cardiac exercise involved walking slowly to the far end of our very short cul de sac, then back again. Once at first, then more often each day. After the first of these pathetically scaled walks Molly came to realise that they were, by her lights, pointless, so she simply sat looking confused in the turning circle and waited for me to come back.

As weeks passed our walks got longer, until that special day when the wife allowed me to go up onto the downs behind the house on my own, with the Moll. I don't know whether she felt anything different about the view that day, but it was magical to me.

Together we progressed to longer and longer walks in Sussex, and eventually I decided that the two of us deserved some quality time together before I returned to work – the two of us, that's Molly and I, by the way. I took her off via one night's stay on the Gower peninsula for a week's walking in Ireland. I remember the Gower because, even after I'd eaten an evening meal at the hotel, I was starving. It was the smallest piece of fish I'd ever seen on a plate and I had to ask the waiter to help me find it. I couldn't bring myself to pay for another meal at the hotel and there was nowhere else. In the end I do hereby confess that Molly's packet of Bonios proved too much of a temptation when I was back in my room and verily I did succumb. I assumed they would taste of nothing very much, like Ryvita, but they were distinctly unpleasant and I think I would have to be in some extremis to repeat the experience. Mind you, I did get through them, which is more than I ever managed with a Hershey bar. So, that's another three advertising campaigns I won't be asked to contribute to.

In my experience dogs are keen to get out and about but they're even more eager to return to the security and familiarity of home, or a surrogate for home. If we took Molly on a long journey by road and stopped at a service station she would always be visibly relieved to return to the car, even if, as in Ireland on our walking holiday, this meant the hire car. And each night in various hotels, as I switched off the bedside light, I would immediately hear the sound of canine claws approaching across the floor, to be followed by a thorough face licking as Molly reassured herself that she wasn't about to be deserted.

We took the car on the ferry from Fishguard to Rosslare and returned Dun Laoghaire to Holyhead, though a rough crossing on the way back caused Molly to throw up badly as well as getting the runs in the back of the car. Don't you just love 'em? But walking in Ireland, north and south, and all the accompanying eating and drinking, was a delight and the presence of Molly guaranteed conversation with the locals and other walkers. Although my focus was on the walking, she did that essentially Labrador thing whenever she saw or smelt water and would race joyously towards it before belly-flopping from a great height like a dog in a cartoon.

A year after Ireland, we repeated our man-and-his-dog week but this time in the Lake District and Molly more or less swam across the national park from one side to the other, tugging unfeasibly sized branches with her.

In complete contrast to a lifelong and determined reluctance to be bathed or hosed down, swimming had always been Molly's "thing" since her first day with us. I had been left in charge of the brand new pup and was quietly reading in the garden when

I heard a loud and worrying splash from the pond. Much to the irritation no doubt of its permanent inmates, the pond was to prove a refuge for Molly throughout her life whenever she became overheated. She could sniff out water at a thousand paces and nothing would prevent her from hurling herself in. Her first big swim was in Loch Lomond near my parents in law and, living in Sussex, she made good use of the sea, especially at the mouth of the Cuckmere River alongside the Seven Sisters cliffs.

She was certainly familiar with the currents and eddies of the River Ouse, which flows through Lewes. We tried to take her in a hired rowing boat on the river at Barcombe above Lewes, but she simply used the boat as a launching pad to the water, to the amusement of the pub customers. She also spotted me taking part in the annual Lewes to Newhaven raft race down the Ouse on a home-made creation decorated to a "British seaside holiday" theme by a group of us from our local babysitting network (we may have been stately in our progress but we did win the prize for best-dressed raft). One sighting of me from the bank and Molly swiftly joined the rafting party in midstream to convoy with us down the river.

I made a full recovery from my cardiac troubles and, though it took a year from start to finish, I was eventually back at work with the County Council on a full-time basis. Perhaps I had lost some momentum, perhaps I had begun not to care quite so much, but when, at an office Christmas party a year or two later, a colleague asked me what had been my work highlight of the year, I spent the whole evening failing to think of one. I was finding it increasingly hard, working in the local authority sector and trying to meet the public's ever growing expectations with fewer and fewer resources. I don't hold this against them – some of my best friends are members of the public. But, when people complained about some service or other being reduced, I would occasionally write pointing out that this was inevitable as the budget and staff had been taken away. I was informed from on high that this was an inappropriate and unprofessional way to respond. I decided to call it a day and handed in my notice.

Less than a week later I was told about a job advert for a part-time post with an environmental charity called the South Downs Society, the unofficial "Friends" group for the South Downs National Park which was in the process of being set up, a mere 60 years after it was first proposed (you can't rush these things). The deadline for job applications was the very next day. I submitted one, was interviewed and was fortunate enough to get the job, which involves working with our member volunteers to lobby on planning, landscape and recreation issues in the national park.

I'm still with the Society and loving every minute of it. I believe, as the respected national park society for the South Downs, we carry out a very valuable function. There will always be lobbying on the national park decision makers to give ground to development pressures from house builders and others and it's essential that groups like us are there hassling them from the other side. Someone has to take a long-term view and not allow our precious landscapes and irreplaceable assets to succumb to all the latest demands and fads. As an organisation we've been around since 1923, so we like to think we're beginning to get the hang of it.

The Society had campaigned vigorously for years in favour of creating the national park. I had been required in my previous job at the County Council to present their case at a major public inquiry *against* setting up the park. By way of introducing me to the Society through the in-house magazine I was asked if I could pen a few words about myself and say something positive about the creation of the national park in case the members were worrying about just where I was coming from! I was also asked to supply an appropriate photograph of myself, so they got one of Molly and me on one of our regular downs walks.

Leaving my full time job with the County Council provided the opportunity to get stuck into a project which had arisen a year or so earlier.

I talked in Chapter 2 about the strangely neglected and unappreciated conurbation of Greater Grotton, nestling, if conurbations can be said to nestle, at the western foot of the Pennines, that very useful mountain range that separates Yorkshire from the civilized world. Our original book "The Grotton Papers: Planning in Crisis" had come out in 1979. Performances around the country by the Grotton Roadshow had continued into the 1980s and the abolition in 1986 of our employer, the Greater Manchester Council, had provided an opportunity for one last rousing rendition of Stand By Your Plan and Grotton, Grotton, Fairest City sung to the tune of Deutschland Uber Alles. There was scarcely a moist eye in the house.

Since that time the Grotton team had gone our separate ways, geographically as well as jobwise. Contact between us had dwindled, as it does, to the odd Christmas card (kids, ask your parents) and vague promises to try to meet up in 1991/1992/1993/2006. It was therefore somewhat out of the blue that I was phoned by one of my fellow Grottonians/old Grotties asking whether I might be up for a second book on the Fairest City, a retrospective as it were. Our professional planners' institute, who had been very supportive of Grotton thirty years earlier, had already interested a publisher and indeed the approach had come from them rather than us having to sell the idea. This is a huge bonus when you're thinking of spending a year or two of your life bashing out words of (what I am reluctant to call) wisdom.

It sounded like a fun idea to me in my newfound freedom from the grind of full-time work and, after a bit of a struggle to convince our third half, we agreed to meet up. Our incisive geographical and town planning training immediately kicked in and we spent several months establishing just where might be the centre point between our respective homes in Lewes, Bath and Manchester, and how this might affect the availability of cheap advance rail fares on a senior railcard (my colleagues were older than me at the time, and indeed still are).

So, Milton Keynes it was. Or Birmingham. Or both, as it happened.

We worked out that a second book was still viable, just about. Another few years and we might all have left the planning system, or have to work in very large fonts. As it was, we thought we could probably convince ourselves that our disparate careers would add a helpful variety and breadth to what we wanted to write about. My colleagues were, in their own separate ways, more engaged with the formal planning system than I had ever been, but I felt, based on my own salary earning efforts, that there was plenty I could say about wider environmental issues, economic development, transport planning and countryside management. There arose a "creative tension" between the three of us (the wounds are nearly healed and the stitches are due to come out shortly) about precisely what the book should be about, and who would be the appropriate audience. One, in particular, of my colleagues was certain that he was writing for an audience of town planners: I wanted to appeal to a wider public that might occasionally bump into a planner or who thought they might just have met someone who had once had dealings with one. I very much wanted to come up with something that my wife, daughter and friends would read and enjoy. We never resolved this basic issue.

We agonised for months over the "conceit". We knew it just had to be about Grotton again, but what might have happened there in the decades since we'd last visited the place? For example, someone had invented "the environment" during that time, while in our day we'd had to make do with geography. Typing pool supervisors were a thing of the past, now that we had all been empowered to do our own word processing. There were now female chief planning officers, for goodness' sake, and no smoking by the coffee urn. And then there was corporate management.

If any one element of my job in later years came to epitomise the antithesis of a rewarding day's labour, it had to be the world's growing obsession with business planning, policy co-ordinators, vision statements, aims and objectives, strategic plans, performance management, appraisal systems, risk assessment – I could go on, but you get the picture. I swiftly volunteered to take responsibility within the new book for knocking out a first draft of a chapter on my bête noire. This chapter originally went by the working title of Corporate B★ll★★★s. We worked together by circulating drafts via the wonders of email, hacking merrily at each other's efforts. They complained that my early drafts of the chapter on corporate management were somewhat "darker" than the rest of the book and could I perhaps, if not too much trouble, try to lighten it up a little. Just me letting off steam, I guess, after years of frustration.

For the purposes of "Grotton Revisited" we settled on the format of a handbook to accompany a (non-existent, of course) conference held to mark Grotton's epoch-making achievement of being scored "Average with Moderate Prospects of Remaining Average" in the government's local authority league tables. This was clearly something worth celebrating and would come, neatly, precisely 31 years and a few months after the previous book and conference.

Time does of course move on and it would have been unsustainable if we had brought out the same characters as before but thirty years older. Let's be serious now, all too few chief planners tend to still be in harness in their nineties, whatever you may allege. Our original hero and Grotton County Planning Officer, Mr T Break, had been replaced painlessly somewhere down the line by his near namesake, Mr Kofi Break. And there was a new Director of Transport and Environment, Donald MacDonald, whose grandfather had built the Forth Bridge, whose father had widened the M5 and whose mother had dug the Mersey Tunnel.

My departure from the County Council – the real one – afforded me the time to press on with this magnum opus. All three of us were still gainfully employed in our respective parts of the country but on a part-time basis, and eventually we had our scribblings available for the publishers' inspection. The book came out in 2010 and I can confidently assure you that it is undoubtedly the finest satirical work ever published about town planning. Indeed, it is almost certainly the only satirical work ever published about town planning, which gives us a head start.

Life has a habit of course of dumping on you from a great height just when you've got something positive going on.

Daughter Mairi had finished at secondary school and, before starting at university, had taken a gap year, the way they do. She may well be the only gap year student to have spent time in both Belize and Vietnam without knowing where either of those places actually was. With my geography background this is a terrible thing to have to admit. Is there an actual thing, "spatial dyslexia"? The journey between the two countries included a flight from California across the Pacific and a change of planes at Taipei, the capital of Taiwan. Mairi and her gap year friend and travelling companion had booked an overnight stay in Taipei because of the twenty-six hour transfer time between flights. On arrival in Taipei they discovered that they had in fact just two hours to make the next flight to Hanoi, their own timings having made no allowance for having crossed the International Date Line on the flight from America. Speed was suddenly of the essence and they never did get to see Taipei.

Anyway, in her second year at university Mairi became extremely ill, and there was no humour in that, for anyone. She turned up on the parental doorstep one Mothers' Day in horrendous pain. There has never been a satisfactory identification of the cause, but we would put good money on it having been triggered by an acute dental abscess and the extraction of a wisdom tooth. Certainly the one followed the other in rapid succession, but none of the relevant medical staff were willing to confirm the link. All we knew for certain was that a formerly bright, socially popular twenty-one year old was permanently suffering from acute and continuous facial and head pain, frequently screaming in what can be reasonably described as agony and the frustration of there being no apparent escape. I took to sleeping on her floor and Margaret and I rearranged our work around her care. It was necessary to separate one's working life from one's home life and, in Margaret's case, to continue to provide a professional level of veterinary service to concerned clients while under the most enormous stress herself. Mairi called a more or less complete halt to any social life or contact with friends from university and for many months was reluctant even to leave the house.

This is not the place for a more detailed account of her travails but I will mention our contact with the social benefits system. For a few months we were able to secure some limited financial assistance for her upkeep while she was unable either to work or study. This, however, did not last. She was obliged, with our help, to complete a benefits assessment form and undergo various interviews – all fair enough in principle, but the questions about capacity to work were restricted to areas like whether she could raise her arm above shoulder height and thereby be up for shelf packing. She wasn't able truthfully to reply no to a single question and was therefore a million miles from eligibility for assistance, despite constant and acute pain levels making any employment quite unrealistic. At this time, one or two of the tabloid newspapers were running front page articles on how the government's welcome crackdown on benefit cheats was yielding massive savings on the grounds that, once obliged to justify their "bogus" claims for assistance through the assessment form and interview, many simply stopped claiming. Mairi, presumably, was one of them.

Writing this book, we are more than four years on from the start of Mairi's illness. Much to our delight she has been back at university for two years, has managed to complete her undergraduate course and once again has a social life to die for. She is still frequently in considerable pain, which has to be managed, but we move forward. Recalling that Mothers' Day in 2009 marked the onset of Mairi's illness, you can be sure that no future Mothers' Day is likely to go unnoticed.

Margaret, you may recall, had changed jobs and was now working with a different local practice. The cases she sees continue to range from the touching to the frankly bizarre, and I get to hear about many of them!

Two elderly ladies arrived for their appointment with an equally ancient and huge Pyrenean Mountain Dog. Until recently it had been in generally good health for a dog of twelve but turned out to be suffering from a badly-infected womb and its prospects didn't look good. Surgery, and the removal of the womb under general anaesthetic, was the only possible solution but, with a bitch of that age, success was far from guaranteed. One of the women, the sister of the bitch's owner, took Margaret on one side and whispered, "You must appreciate that Snowy is all she's got. Since her husband died, she's all she lives for. I know you'll do your best". So, no pressure then.

It proved the trickiest of operations, and a lengthy one. But the dog came round OK, the op had clearly been successful and Snowy was able to go home.

Just over a year later the sister was back at the surgery with her own cat and brought Margaret up to date. Snowy's owner had been delighted of course to see her dog safely returned to her but had herself died recently at the age of ninety two. Snowy died just four days later.

Indeed it is not unusual for an elderly pet to "call it a day" almost immediately after its owner, perhaps struggling with a prolonged illness, has passed away. One might be forgiven for believing that either the animal dies of a broken heart or it feels its duty is done and its therapeutic services are no longer needed.

One ageing cat being seen by the practice was the sole companion of an equally elderly woman. The pair were clearly inseparable and probably contributing to each other's longevity. Eventually the woman was taken into residential care in her declining years. Normally such care homes tend to exclude pets but, when apprised of the closeness of the relationship, this one relented and the cat was allowed to accompany her owner into the home, where the two lived on contentedly for several more years. When the woman died, the cat was brought into the surgery facing the possibility of euthanasia, never having really known any other companion. As fortune would have it, the practice knew of another elderly woman who had just lost her own very old cat and she was more than happy to offer a home to the bereaved puss. Last heard, the pair were still providing vital mutual support!

Another client came into the surgery with a young female cat which appeared to be putting on a significant amount of weight and displaying a number of behavioural changes. After a clinical examination and obtaining a detailed case history the vet informed the owner that there was nothing untoward happening, the cat was simply pregnant. This diagnosis was briskly dismissed by the client:

"No, that can't be true. It must be something else."

"But the signs are clear. Why do you think she can't be pregnant?"

"She's a house cat. She never goes out. She wouldn't ever meet another cat."

"And you have no other cats in the house? Didn't you bring in a different cat a few weeks ago?"

"Don't be silly, that's her brother!"

Meanwhile Margaret had been treating a black curly-haired poodle belonging to a middle-aged female client, also with tightly curled, dyed black hair. Well, you know what they say about dogs and their owners...

The client was in the surgery to collect a prescription for a gastric upset.

"Ah, Miss Taylor," said Margaret, "how has she been? How's the paw?"

"Her paws have been fine."

"And the eye?"

"Her eyes are just fine, thank you".

A month later the curly-haired lady and the curly-haired poodle appeared back in the surgery.

"Hallo Miss Taylor. Everything all right? How have her bowel movements been? Stools OK?"

With a slightly puzzled expression, the lady replied "Her insides are absolutely fine, thank you, but that eye thing has flared up again".

At which point one of the veterinary nurses motioned to Margaret to step out into the corridor.

"You do know there are two Miss Taylors? Twins. They both have poodles?"

Wildlife can bring its own veterinary issues. Our own garden backs onto a small copse and we are fortunate enough, despite our pets, to enjoy the presence of a variety of birdlife. Like many people we make efforts to put obstacles in the way of the grey squirrels so that the birds can have a fair shot at the seeds and other goodies on the bird table. Squirrels of course tend to be adept at finding their way round, through, over or under whatever you put in front of them. All except one – we assumed it was always the same one – that had a tendency to lose its footing when under pressure and descend to earth in an ungainly manner. "Mister Clumsy", as we named it, always came back for more.

One day, watching through the kitchen window and amused by its efforts, we saw it land on the ground with a bump, and there it stayed. Margaret checked it out. The intrepid commando was clearly concussed, but there were no obvious fractures and we popped it in a box and brought it indoors to recover. An hour or two later when we checked on it, the squirrel had clearly regained consciousness and seemed raring to go. We briefly contemplated putting up a safety net for it as it returned to the garden to renew its battle with the obstacle course.

Members of the public will often bring into the vet's surgery an injured bird or wild animal they have come across in the house or garden or by the roadside. Of course they tend to feel that they have done their good deed by taking the trouble to bring the wounded creature in. They don't expect to pay for the treatment, or euthanasia, and this may be covered by the practice or by some local group. People will sometimes be tempted to pick up and "rescue" a fledgling that they assume to have been abandoned. RSPB advice would be generally to leave well alone – the parent birds may well be close by.

Margaret was presented one day with a small box containing a stunned robin, seemingly the victim of an attack by a cat. One eye was closed, the other eye socket was covered in blood, and the bird was clearly suffering from shock. There was a real prospect that the bird had lost an eye. But, after a period of quiet and gentle bathing of the bloodied area, it was clear that the robin had suffered only a minor wound. It managed eventually to open both eyes and Margaret carried the bird to the back door of the surgery to release it. The robin sat for a few seconds on her open hand, tilting its head from side to side and seeming to observe her, before flying away. Margaret felt she had been afforded a moment of privilege by one of nature's little celebrities. By way of comparison, the occasional injured gull, no doubt fresh from the local landfill site and brought to the surgery in a cardboard box or cat basket, looks the size of a condor at close range and has a beak that could shred a motorway crash barrier.

Hedgehogs, despite Beatrix Potter's Mrs. Tiggy-Winkle spin, are not all that cuddly and they are rarely to be seen in true life doing the ironing. They have spines and fleas and they can bite. They are also frequent visitors to the vets' as a result of encounters with cars, pets and bonfires or being found worse for wear and riddled with maggots. Their little piggy snuffles are a not infrequent sound in the surgery. Of course, in rolling up into a tight defensive ball, they possess a built-in protective mechanism which prevents medical assistance being readily given. To prise the hedgehog ball open the vet will often insert a tube and pass a small amount of oxygen and anaesthetic gas through it with a view to relaxing the hedgehog and rendering it capable of being uncurled so it can be examined.

If this were an illustrated book it would definitely include at least one photograph of a hedgehog suffering from "balloon syndrome". One was brought to Margaret's surgery having been found in the garden with this condition. Bacteria infecting a wound may give rise to a build up of gas under the skin. The hedgehog then "blows up" like a football with spines on. Incapable of curling up, it is visually more suited to being bounced. The vet was able to release the gas, deflate the hedgehog (and no, it didn't fly up to the ceiling and around the room, this is serious), clean the wound and treat it with a course of antibiotics. The creature made a full recovery.

While hedgehogs tend to come off worse in clashes with cars, the same may also be said about dogs that try abseiling down cliffs without the aid of a safety harness. Living as we now do in Sussex in proximity to Beachy Head, the Seven Sisters and other high points of the south coast, it is not unusual to hear of, or see at the surgery, examples of unaided bungee jumping by dogs which were too preoccupied by clearing the cliff top of birdlife or undertaking the essential task of frisbee retrieval. On one occasion, walking Molly, our black Labrador, along the line of the "Sisters" from Cuckmere Haven, I spotted her sprinting in the direction of an unsuspecting gull which just happened to be standing within one yard (nearly a metre for any youngsters reading) of the cliff edge. The fact that my normally calm, reasoning vocal approach to her was in this instance replaced by an ear piercing scream did the trick, she slammed on the brakes and came to the kind of furrow ploughing stop you usually see only in cartoons. It is true that some paragliding canines survive the drop but you wouldn't want to bank on it.

Sometimes the dinner table conversation at the vet's house can be quite uplifting.

A local couple brought a two-year-old black and white female cat into the surgery looking, at first glance, more or less beyond recall (the cat, that is, not the couple). They had an extraordinary tale to tell. Their friends and next door neighbours had moved house some six months earlier from Sussex to somewhere in Scotland for the father's job. The family cat had gone missing almost immediately after they arrived in Scotland and, despite the family touring the area, knocking on doors and putting up "wanted" posters, it wasn't seen again.

Until, that is, the couple now standing in front of Margaret had looked out of the window into their own back garden and spotted a black and white cat which could just, if she had been carrying twice the weight, been a double for the one that used to live next door. The animal was dehydrated, emaciated and clearly in a very bad way. They managed to bring her into the house and phoned their former neighbours to ask if their cat was safely accounted for. This of course triggered astonishment at the other end of the phone line – the children and their parents had all been distraught at the loss.

The cat was freezing cold, almost comatose. Having inspected her, Margaret concluded that, sadly, she was too far gone and that euthanasia was really the best option. The owners in Scotland, however, when contacted, urged that everything possible should be done to save the refugee, whatever the financial cost, and, against her better judgement, the vet acceded to their request.

The cat was unable to take normal food. She was placed on a heat pad, put on a drip and fed intravenously. There was no apparent response for nearly 48 hours and the possibility of euthanasia again arose. But, on the third day, a faint 'miaow' was heard by one of the veterinary nurses and the cat showed signs of attempting to raise its head. She was eventually able to lap a little milk, then take more solid food from a fingertip. The next day she managed to rise unsteadily to her feet, purred and wondered what all the fuss was about.

I was given daily updates on its progress and couldn't wait for each evening's instalment. Indeed, my own colleagues responded in similar vein. If it happened today the cat would have her own Facebook account or Twitter feed. The owners were of course on the phone every day from Scotland. After five or six days the cat was making up for lost time, eating everything put in front of her and purring non-stop. The family made arrangements to drive down for a reunion with their pet.

With strict instructions from the vet, they took the cat back with them and ensured that she didn't step outside the house for several months to avoid any repeat. The delighted owners reported that she had settled into her new environment in Scotland, regained her fluff and recovered her previous body weight. They sent a photograph to show how well she was doing. One can only assume that any further house moves by the family will have to be very carefully considered, then abandoned.

This may be the only recorded case of the wife admitting she was wrong. The cat itself is unavailable for comment but is understood to be negotiating her own book deal.

Clients of course come in all shapes and sizes. There was the woman who rang Margaret's surgery to say that her husband had succeeded in trapping the cat's tail in a door, it had come off and should she bring the tail in with her for reattachment. She would get there as soon as she could, but at the moment she was dealing with the husband, who had passed out on the bathroom floor.

A middle-aged man brought a male cat in to be neutered and asked, while it was anaesthetised, if its matted fur might be teased out – not always easy with a sensitive cat. When he returned to the surgery later that day he was informed that all had gone according to plan and the cat was ready to be taken home.

"Did you manage to remove his knots?" he quizzed the young, new receptionist.

"Pardon?" she replied, somewhat taken aback.

"His knots. Did you get rid of them?"

"Absolutely" she replied, checking the case notes. "That's what he came in for!"

At which point one of the veterinary nurses leant across and whispered, "He's asking about his knots, dear, not his nuts."

There is a skill in explaining quite complex medical terms and procedures to the layman, it being important to convey the nature of the illness, likely prognosis and intended treatment in a comprehensible manner.

"Timmy will need an operation so first we're going to *an-aes-thet-ise* him – that means give him a general *an-aes-thet-ic*" explained Margaret slowly and clearly to a worried looking elderly gent who had brought in his Cocker Spaniel for treatment. "He'll go to sleep, just for a while, so he won't feel a thing. First we put a kind of fine needle, that we call a catheter, into a V-E-I-N in his front leg, then we insert what we vets call an endotracheal tube into his W-I-N-D-P-I-P-E which will deliver the anaesthetic G-A-S to keep him asleep so he'll feel no pain during the O-P-E-R-A-T-I-O-N."

The old man only nodded gently and thanked Margaret very much for explaining it so well and putting him at ease.

"You know who that was?" said a grinning nurse as he left. "He's been a client for about ten years. He's a Fellow of the Royal College of Anaesthetists and I think he's Professor of Anaesthesia at one of the London medical schools. I think he was able to follow you all right".

Happily both the anaesthetic and the operation were a success.

The run up to Bonfire Night is a busy one for most veterinary practices round the country, and nowhere more so than anywhere within striking distance of our town of Lewes in East Sussex. Many pets become very disturbed by the sudden noises and flashes and the owners will seek any possible remedy or mitigation. Indeed Margaret wrote an article for a local lifestyle magazine on this very subject.

For reasons of history and tradition which are varied and complicated, Lewes has become the centre of bonfire celebrations that are the largest in the country. (Sorry Shetland, we both loved Up Helly Aa but Lewes is bigger, I'm afraid). On November the 5th crowds of up to 50,000 flock to a town of only 16,000 population to watch or take part in over thirty costumed, torch-bearing processions to half a dozen separate huge bonfires, accompanied by massive aerial firework displays and the ceremonial burning of tableaux and effigies. Pet friendly it isn't. Through October each year Margaret calmly and professionally advises clients on how best to counter this awful assault on their pets' eardrums and nerves. And on the 5th she dons her Commercial Square Bonfire Society yellow and black striped "smugglers" jersey and strides out with the rest of Lewes to the sound of Sussex by the Sea or the nearest salsa band, hurling fire crackers and crow scarers with the best of them. Her shameful secret. Hey ho.

Every veterinary practice affords unlimited opportunities for mayhem, embarrassment and offbeat humour.

My nephew Sam, working in the same practice in Northumberland as his dad, reported the case of an irritating, smart, image-conscious woman arriving late for her dog's appointment and bringing a second Chihuahua to be treated at the same time because she "presumed that's allowed". One of the patients, being a little temperamental, tried to bite the nasty vet. The client scooped it up to comfort her poor baby, but in so doing she managed to place her hand over the dog's rear end and, in the process, smeared diarrhoea over it. When stressed, the woman had the unfortunate mannerism of running her hands through her hair so when Sam pointed out the mess on her hand, she immediately wiped it over the side of her head. When this in turn was pointed out, she repeated the action. Sam started to feel so much better about having been kept waiting.

Another client was in the habit of travelling up from County Durham with assorted gerbils, hamsters and voles but, although she was a regular customer, she never seemed impressed with the treatment offered. One day she brought a box full of shavings containing an off-colour Steppe Lemming. Now, I can confirm that all vets develop a proficiency at the "hamster flick", separating the end of one's finger from the teeth of said rodent by... well, it speaks for itself. In this case, having made painful contact with the lemming while rummaging through the box of shavings, Sam performed his own version of the flick. On this occasion, instead of the normal splat against the ceiling, he dived forward and caught it perfectly, inches from the ground. The client stood open-mouthed and all Sam could say was, "Now, you've *got* to be impressed by that!" From then on, she would invariably bring a friend with her on visits to the vet in the hope of a repeat performance. Sam still failed to cure any of her animals.

A colleague – Sam insists it wasn't him – was carrying out a consultation on a dog on an old table with drawers. The drawers were handy for storing cotton wool and other materials which might be useful during the consultation. One of the other vets had also found one of the drawers to be a useful receptacle for a gerbil which she'd put to sleep earlier and intended to take through to the mortuary at the end of the surgery. Our heroine was required to empty the dog's anal glands. She put on a latex glove and reached for the cotton wool while holding up the dog's tail with the other hand. She continued to chat with the client, who started to look very concerned before asking, "Where were you planning on putting that?" while indicating the dead rodent in her glove.

Sam had spent his first year's work, post-qualification, at a practice in Skipton – believing (wisely, one would have thought) that it made sense to commit all his beginner's errors somewhere other than the Northumberland practice where he hoped to build a career and where his father was a partner. Being the new boy he was therefore fair game for having some of the more "interesting" clients dumped on him.

The receptionist rang through with a call from a client who had been feeling under the weather and wondered if this could be related to the fact that he had been treating his dog with Frontline flea drops.

Sam: "Hello Mr X, I understand you've been feeling sick after treating your dog with Frontline – can I ask when that was?"

Client: "I put it on him two weeks ago, stroked him a couple of hours later and was feeling grotty yesterday."

Sam: "Well, it's more of an issue for your doctor than your vet, but Frontline has a wide safety margin and it seems very unlikely it would cause sickness in you, especially after two weeks."

Client: "It's not really sickness. The thing is – it's my testicles. They've swollen to a phenomenal size - could that be the Frontline?"

Sam: "I really think you need to consult your doctor."

Client: "But is it the Frontline?"

Sam: "I doubt it very much."

Client: "Oh, OK. No worries then. Thanks mate."

Sam: "What do you mean 'no worries'? You're telling me that your testicles have swollen to a phenomenal size. Go and see your doctor!"

In the background one of the partners who had been listening in, waved and smiled as he headed towards the toilets brandishing a bottle of Frontline spray.

Client: "Nah. It'll be all right. Thanks anyway."

The nature of "foreign bodies" retrieved from animals' insides, particularly dogs, continues to impress. Since all dogs are descended from pack-dwelling ancestors when feeding time was a free for all, the dog evolved to eat first and ask questions afterwards on the basis that what is in his stomach is safely his. If horribly contaminated or otherwise unsuitable, it can always be vomited up at a later date. When this doesn't work, a foreign body may be the outcome.

The veterinary nurses, having carried out their own brief external examination, will often run a sweepstake on what will eventually be removed by the vet on the operating table.

"Hard and round. I reckon that's got to be a ball".

"I'm going for a stone. It's about time we had another stone."

"Mm. Remember it's a Setter. Could be a light bulb like the last one."

One might assume that the object most frequently removed from the dog's digestive tract would be a bone, but in practice these tend to come some way down the list. Small objects imbued with body fluids seem irresistible, so babies' dummies, contraceptives, handkerchiefs and particularly socks loom large in the "body count". If you own a dog and you've mislaid a sock, chances are it's not been swallowed by the washing machine but by the family pet. One Golden Retriever, a frequent visitor to Margaret's surgery, consumed dozens of them, not necessarily at one sitting but on a regular basis.

Sometimes the owner would find it difficult, even sensitive, to advise the vet just what the offending article might be. If Margaret's return phone call to the client was made from home I would occasionally overhear her end of the conversation.

"You think he's swallowed something?...Why do you think he might have swallowed something?...What kind of material?... How big a garment?...Well, how many thongs?"

This one generated a degree of anticipation at the practice before the young female owner came in with the dog, as well as giving rise to a jolly discussion about whether to offer her the "foreign body" back after it had been removed and whether she was likely to want it. They offered. She didn't.

Dogs will basically swallow anything. Margaret has brought home the odd X-ray to show me and the one with a small rubber duck clearly visible probably looked the sweetest. Some of these children's toys are well-nigh indestructible. And Superglue, of course, presents its own challenges.

The list of objects she has recovered over the years from patients' insides runs to squash balls, rocks, needles, corn cobs (especially in the barbecue season), curtain rings, sticks, coins, knives and forks, a mobile phone, CDs, specs, a necklace and even dentures, though my favourite would have to be a pair of rubber underpants. And that was one that the owner definitely struggled with. He explained that they "belonged to a friend" who had "accidentally left them".

The dog may of course eventually just pass the offending article and the owner will have the chance to recover the missing ring, or whatever, but otherwise it's a case of the vet extracting it "endoscopically", by insertion of a slender "grab", or by opening the animal up under general anaesthetic.

Dogs also consume their owners' medication on a regular basis, sometimes still in the pill box. Of course, for the vet to be able to treat the affected animal, the owner needs to come clean on just what drug the dog has taken, whatever its legality. There have been a good few pets brought to the surgery over the years under the influence of cannabis and one Bull Terrier, brought in by a short man with impressive muscles, had swallowed some growth hormone apparently banned from national bodybuilding competitions. When Margaret contacted the Poisons Helpline, they queried the source of the drug but they did furnish the necessary advice.

She looked forward with interest to the anticipated arrival of an allegedly intelligent Dalmatian that had digested an entire volume of the Encyclopaedia Britannica, 2010 edition, but this turned out to be a hoax by a colleague. Which is all you need.

For the purposes of this book I asked my brother what had been the most interesting swallowed items he had encountered over his years as a vet. He mentioned a woman who brought in her cat together with a dog's tail, all that remained of a friend's Chihuahua she had been looking after until her own pet had unfortunately viewed it as some sort of tasty rodent. But, in terms of an actual foreign body requiring surgery, he said that would probably be a Cliff Richard tape. A black band could be seen under the tongue of a German Shepherd brought to the surgery. This proved to be a loop of cassette tape caught around the tongue, then passing down the oesophagus. Opening up the stomach had enabled him to free more of the tape but further lengths passed into the small intestine. Further incisions enabled him to free yet more tape but he was dismayed to find the furthest end of the cassette passed through the narrow junction between intestine and colon, necessitating a final incision to free the last four inches from the rectum. As the nurse had said at the time, "Summer Holiday at the mouth, Bachelor Boy in the stomach, Young Ones in the bowel and CONGRATULATIONS at the bum!"

CHAPTER NINE

FARMING CAMELS AND THE FINAL FRONTIER

"Oh, you can get lonely. And a cat's no help with that"
Pet Shop Boys, I Want a Dog

"For me euthanasia would be the best thing"
Veterinary medicine lecture, 1980

Family visits to my brother's farm in Northumberland have continued throughout our time in Sussex. We arrived on one occasion to find a badger occupying the kitchen. He had been brought to my brother's veterinary practice as the victim of a road traffic accident ("RTA") and John was allowing Ratbag, as he had been nicknamed, to recuperate from surgery at the farm before being released back into the wild.

The family dogs were clearly unimpressed and wisely gave Ratbag a wide berth whenever he stirred himself. He would suddenly launch into an exploration of the kitchen cupboards, scattering pans and crockery in all directions before tackling the potted plants. He was clearly less biddable than the dogs.

During his R and R at the farm Ratbag had become accustomed to being with people, and I was invited to pick him up and "give him a cuddle". I have a photo of me holding Ratbag in my arms and you couldn't call it relaxed. I was very conscious that his teeth were just a few inches from my jugular.

Outside in the farmyard, John had done his best to create a badger-proof compound. It would be undesirable for the injured animal to escape before the vet felt he was ready. Ratbag would spend his days patrolling the perimeters like a Colditz escape committee, testing the barricades for any points of weakness. One could guess how the word "badgering" came to mean what it does.

John was in touch with a local badger group who were keen to identify an appropriate sett to which Ratbag might reasonably be returned. It doesn't do, apparently, to leave a single badger, and one not necessarily in the best condition, totally isolated in the countryside, nor in a well-populated and possibly hostile badger community. But while these discussions were taking place Ratbag took the law into his own hands and, while the searchlights and guards were looking the other way, made good his escape. No postcard was ever received to indicate safe arrival.

The farm provided an admirable venue for family gatherings. Major family events like birthdays or engagement parties brought large numbers of guests to be accommodated in outbuildings or in a tented village in one of the fields. John's daughter Nicky - my niece – had her wedding reception at the farm, with the entire guest list strolling back from the village church together. Hospitality was always on a grand scale at the farm and that day it included a huge sit-down wedding breakfast in a marquee, a hog roast and a barn dance.

We partied into the early hours but, as the last guests started to head to their billets, one reported back that there were a couple of wallabies on the loose from their own paddock. Without more ado, and knowing well that most of the guests would be incapable of doing what was required, the bride girded up her wedding dress, put on a pair of wellies and set off with a determined look on her face. In such instances, experience counts for a lot.

Her mother had made up a splendid bower in the loft of one of the loose boxes for Nicky and her new husband, Ed, to spend their wedding night. Amongst the rabbits, catering packs of bread rolls and ketchup and large bags of animal feedstuff, and with doves cooing above, they were able to pass a first night of wedded bliss. Mother had unfortunately bolted the door from the outside last thing before she turned in herself. So, when nature called during the night, as it will after that much drink, Nicky had to persuade her new hubby to exit the loft via a hatch door in the roof and scale the outside of the building to let her out.

As a thank you gift to John and Shelagh for the wedding and much else besides, Nicky and Ed had imported a young Bactrian camel from Austria (Austria! I know!) to replace the recently deceased dromedary, Gloria. Well, you can't have a decent farm without a camel, can you? Gabby – the new arrival - had proved impossible to gift wrap (no, don't tell me, is it a CD?) but had been safely concealed at Nicky's brother Sam's place in the same village. Made our set of kitchen knives look pretty damned ordinary as a wedding present, that's all I'm saying.

Gabby has risen to the not inconsiderable challenge of standing in for Gloria at the village nativity play. Indeed it would be hard to imagine anybody/anything else in the village auditioning for the part. The farmyard and associated buildings serve as a splendid setting for the local community's celebration of the Christmas story, incorporating such staples as lowing llamas, shepherds guarding their wallabies and angels hoisted high on a forklift truck. If the neighbourhood kids can't buy into that lot, then it's a poor do.

The winter of 2008 was marked by a major flood in the middle of Morpeth, where John's main veterinary surgery was located. The River Wansbeck overflowed its banks and the single-storey surgery was immediately threatened. John had set off to fetch sandbags but, with the waters rising swiftly, he was unable to get back into town. His wife Shelagh, son Sam – by this time a partner in the practice – and various other vets, nurses and reception staff rapidly arranged for the owners of the pets being kept in the building for treatment to remove their animals if at all possible. A house owned by the practice and occupied by an employee lay just across the road and was, importantly, two storeys. With flood waters rising to waist level, the lifeboat service began ferrying vital medical equipment, computers and the remaining pets in cages and kennels across the car park and street to safety upstairs. By the later stages of this process, the water was too deep to wade through and their rescuers were swimming alongside their modern day ark.

While undoubtedly the most dramatic element, this was only one step in a long haul. The floodwaters had put paid to the electrics in the house across the road, so Shelagh and Sam passed the whole of that night in the dark with their flock and with no source of power.

We have all watched the scenes on the TV news as exhausted-looking householders begin the long, heartbreaking process of cleaning up after a flood. This was the inevitable next step for the practice. Equipment needed to be replaced, as did fittings and furnishings. The practice was fortunate to have a number of smaller branch surgeries in nearby towns, and so, with huge effort from all concerned, was able to maintain its business and client base in a cutthroat commercial world. They were back in the main Morpeth surgery by summer 2009.

This would also be an appropriate time to mention the strange story of the family's blue, yellow and green macaw, Robinson. It would have been fun to describe Robinson as having escaped the flooding from the River Wansbeck perched on the shoulder of a lifeboat man. But it wouldn't have been true. Robinson lived at the farm, not the surgery, and had done so for some twenty years. He had had his wings clipped long since and didn't fly. He generally lived in or around the farmhouse kitchen, sitting atop his cage and occasionally waking himself from a long snooze to take a mean-spirited peck at people daring to walk past. On fine days he was allowed outside where he walked the walls and fence lines and could cover a fair distance.

One day Robbie was grabbed from the garden in broad daylight by a group of hoodied youngsters who obviously knew he was there. They were clearly visible on the farm's CCTV and before long the local police had identified and charged most, though not all, of the culprits.

John's family had regarded Robinson much as the rest of us regard our cat or dog. He had after all been a member of that family for two decades. They decided to offer a reward for his recovery, though conscious that if the stolen bird should become too "hot", his life might be put at greater risk. It felt worse not knowing where he was, or how he was being treated.

A year passed.

Into the post-flood renovated Morpeth surgery came a couple seeking treatment for a brightly-coloured macaw which they called Robbie. They had paid £800 for him and decided to call him Robbie as that's what he kept saying. An alert nurse, thinking she might have recognised the macaw from her own pet-minding stints at the farm, removed the bird to another room, invented an excuse to keep him in overnight and the police were informed. Nobody was in any doubt that Robinson had come home.

Once the couple were cleared of any direct connection with the theft, they were understandably miffed at losing both their new pet and their £800 but there was reluctance to offer them either visiting rights or the full reward, as they hadn't come forward in response to any appeal. What exactly Robinson thought of the whole affair has not been established. He's back home on the farm, once more squawking unpleasantly and still trying to take lumps out of passers-by. And I still hate him.

After all the effort of getting the Morpeth surgery up and running again after the 2008 flood, it was only to remain in business for a further three years. It occupied a prime town centre site and was coveted by a national supermarket chain. Following compulsory purchase by the local council, the practice was offered compensation to enable it to relocate to a new site on the outskirts of the town.

The new £3.5 million state-of-the-art centre, designed externally to simulate a Northumbrian farmstead, was opened in 2012. It houses an extraordinary array of treatment facilities and employs around fifteen vets, plus nursing, administration and reception staff. John's wife, Shelagh, is now the practice manager while Sam's wife, Lizzy, is finance manager! Now that's what I call letting your other half's work take over your life. I may have spent nights accompanying the wife-vet on her calls, taken copious phone messages about unorthodox canine bowel movements, suffered oral assaults on my preferred diet and seen friends abandon us, but hey, at least I'm not working for her.

That said, and assuming there are no vets reading this, I might just admit to a begrudging admiration for what they do. Margaret, for example, may be incapable of unrolling a length of clingfilm without losing the end of it, and her idea of drying clothes is to leave them in a tight ball overnight and shout at them in the morning, but fair's fair, what the veterinary profession is called on to do each day at work does matter. Nothing dies if I get it wrong in the office.

Along with the half-dozen outlying branch surgeries, the opening of the new centre heralds quite some transformation since my big brother started work in Morpeth in the late 1960s. Then the practice occupied part of the home of the principal partner, where entrance to the surgery was via the rear of the house, operations were performed on a flat wooden top fixed to the hydraulic base of an old dentist's chair and X-rays were carried out after hours at the local cottage hospital. While the practice's preoccupation in the 60s was with farm work, and domestic pets were almost an afterthought, that balance has completely changed, with pet surgeries now running all day, equine work busier than ever and farm animals accounting for a much smaller percentage of the business.

We last met Molly, our black Labrador, assisting my recovery from a dodgy ticker by walking and swimming across Ireland and the Lake District. Despite being a vet's dog she was quite well looked after and remained in rude health until she was at least twelve or thirteen. True, she started to experience stress at having her rear end sniffed when out and about, but that probably goes for most of us. Well into her twelfth winter she was hurtling down the local toboggan run trying to leap on board the family sledge and, once she'd succeeded in overturning it, licking you to death.

But eventually, in her fourteenth year, the wheels really did come off as far as Molly's health was concerned. Various quite serious problems developed including a malignant tumour in her mouth which caused loss of appetite (an extraordinary event with a Labrador and therefore definitely a bad sign) and occasional heavy blood loss, and a reduction in nerve sensitivity in her hindquarters, which left her unpredictable control over the movement of her back legs. Her walks of necessity became shorter and slower and she had to be lifted up and down the front steps and in and out of the car.

During what turned out to be her last summer I walked her along the banks of the River Ouse above Lewes and she was unable to resist her lifelong urge to dive into the river from a high bank. It was quite sweet to see her back in her true element as a reincarnated fish after I had grown used to seeing her look clumsy and unhappy on land, but, when she'd tired of that and headed for the bank, there was no prospect of her getting out. When young this had presented no problem. If she wasn't able to climb back onto the bank, she would swim along until she reached somewhere with a more gentle gradient. This time, however, she clearly didn't possess the strength for a long swim and she had insufficient control of her back legs to stand on the bottom and heave herself up. I briefly thought about trying to pull her up by the collar or shoulders but this trick had failed before and in any event tended to leave both parties exhausted and comprehensively muddied.

There was nothing for it. I stripped to my pants (boxers fortunately, not budgie smugglers) and clambered in. It was deeper than I expected. I was soon in mud and mucky river water to chest level but Molly seemed to approve. At least this made heaving her out relatively straightforward. I decided to walk further along the bank to dry out before putting my clothes back on. So it was sod's law that the first group of walkers who came towards me included in their number a young former colleague (female, naturally) from County Hall.

We took Molly with us for New Year to Margaret's mother's house, close to Loch Lomond where she (the dog) had enjoyed her first proper swim nearly fourteen years earlier. We warned mum-in-law that this might well be the last time Molly would be coming up with us. On New Year's day itself, clearing our heads of any post Hogmanay fuzziness, we drove up to the lochside for a slow dogwalk in the country park. Lifted down from the back of the car, Molly set off with some determination, looking, we assumed, for a convenient place to poo. But she clearly had the scent of the loch in her nostrils and soon launched into as near a full run as might be thought feasible for an ailing thirteen-year-old Labrador. In a throwback to my holidays with her in Ireland and the Lakes, Molly simply raced downhill with Margaret struggling well behind shouting, "Steve, she's going in the loch! Stop her!" And this a dog that had hardly been able to walk for the past nine months or so.

I stood stock still and laughed. But I realised that, however amusing, this was a situation that needed sorting, and I got myself down to the shore of the loch as quickly as I could to haul her out. Both her first and last swims had taken place in Loch Lomond. This was labelled in the family memory as "Molly's last run" – and so it proved.

Margaret's clients tend to pass responsibility for the "last big decision" to the professional. "The vet says it would be kinder to Tyson", they say to the children. But when you're the vet, it's harder to decide when to end the life of a creature that you've shared your home with. In Molly's case she almost faded away in the back of the car on our next trip north to mother in law's, just three months after her "last run". The decision was more or less made for us. I rang Mairi back home in Lewes. She had made it clear that she wished to be present for Molly's last moments, but circumstances wouldn't permit. Through the past few months Margaret had made sure she always had the requisite "bumping juice" to hand and, while I held Molly's head, the deed was done. Molly's eyes never left mine, she didn't move a muscle, and I felt a sadness I hadn't experienced for a long, long time.

Ah well, they said, it's the way she would have wanted to go. She was with her family and somewhere familiar. Personally I'm not so sure about that. I think she might well have preferred, being a Labrador, to bow-wow out while doggy paddling in a vat of chocolate while reeking of fox poo, but there you go.

We had only just arrived in Scotland the previous evening after our trek from Sussex. Being away from home, and having no intention of driving a very dead Molly all the way back to Lewes a few days later, Margaret phoned a local vet, explained the situation and we agreed to take her round to his surgery that morning to arrange for a private cremation (we're as soft as anyone else). I had thought, in the spirit of placing the dog's favourite playthings with her on her final journey, that we might pop Peanuts the ginger tom, then eighteen, in with her, but he was safely some 500 miles away. The cremation wouldn't be taking place until after we'd returned home to Sussex, so Margaret's sister in law, who lives near the vet's in Scotland, agreed to collect the ashes for us a few days later. It was unbelievably sad to leave Molly with another vet and to set off for home without her.

What does one do with all that doggy paraphernalia? I couldn't decide whether to leave the odd Frisbee or mangled tennis ball dotted round the garden by way of souvenir. What would we do now with all those leftovers from the dinner table which Molly had been so skilled at recycling? Would I now be obliged, in her absence, to clean up any future cat's sick rather than leaving it to disappear "through natural processes"? Would the absence of doggy smell encourage uninvited neighbourhood cats through our catflap? (The answer on this one was, annoyingly, yes.)

A few months later, on another trip north, we were able to collect Molly's ashes from Margaret's sister-in-law and bring her home. I wasn't sure of the protocol here. I couldn't recall Molly giving any clear indication of her wishes in respect of her ashes. Margaret felt they should be disposed of in Molly's favourite place. "What? Round the fridge?" I ventured. But Margaret was having none of that. "To Wilderness Wood" she said. Wilderness Wood is a very attractive privately-owned woodland in East

Sussex, open to the public and our Moll's best-loved walk. The wife usually gets her way in these matters, so the Wood it was.

The three human Ankers plus pot set off for a wander along Molly's old, familiar pathways through the wood, scattering a few ashes as we went but saving most for a bridge over a small stream at the very bottom of the wood, at the furthest point from habitation. Alongside the bridge was an open-sided wooden hut thing where we had frequently sat and passed the time of day, known to us as the Blair Witch Hut. I had once suggested to Mairi that she hire it out for an overnight stay. "Go on, I dare you. How much would we have to pay you to spend a night out here on your own?"

But on this day of all days Molly's bridge was, for the first time ever in our experience, surrounded by a large crowd of intruders. They appeared to be a wedding party. Margaret sighed that we wouldn't now be able to dispose of Molly in the way we had planned, but I was made of more determined stuff that day and headed through the throng to the bridge. I decided that if I was asked what I was doing in the middle of someone else's wedding celebrations, I would say it was a Sussex tradition and dab just a little of Molly on the nearest forehead. Just how many wedding pictures we now appear in, I have no idea, but I would like to think there might be the odd puzzled expression when the albums are brought out a few years down the line.

We saved a portion of the ash to scatter on another day – I was really getting the hang of this now – and that meant a downland walk around a circuit behind our house, or Angina

Hill, as I had once known it. We reached a point on the walk where I remembered pausing with Molly the first time we'd been up on the chalk ridge after my heart surgery. It seemed like an ideal place to reflect on the good times. Knowing this was the end of the pot and feeling quite emotional, there was almost a tear in my eye as I tossed the remaining ashes into the air. Unfortunately, caught up with the occasion, I had failed to take on board a late shout from Margaret to check the direction of the wind. What remained of Molly came straight back to land on my face and hair - the kind of thing you think will only happen in a sitcom. For the next day or two I was still spotting vestiges of Molly as the bath water drained out. I just knew she'd never want to leave me.

There was a codicil to this. I was very reluctant to go back to Wilderness Wood after Molly died. The enjoyment of the visit had always been about the sharing of pleasure, and competition for the cakes at the tearoom, with the faithful Labrador. I couldn't now quite get the idea of walking for its own sake. It simply felt weird wandering about in the countryside on my own. What is a chap supposed to do in those circumstances out in the middle of nowhere, sans dog, to reassure any approaching solitary woman of one's good intentions? Anyway, eventually Margaret persuaded me to go back to the Wood and we again wandered down to the Blair Witch Hut by the distant stream. Margaret stepped onto Molly's bridge, looked down to the trickle of water below and jokingly, but sort of tenderly at the same time, called out, "Molly, Molly, are you there? Can you hear me?" At which point we both glimpsed at the corner of our respective eye a young black Labrador, identical to Moll in her younger, fitter years – other than having a noticeably laddish dangly bit, as vets call it. It was a surreal moment. One second there was nothing around but us and our memories, the next we had company, and the dog was clearly looking at us. There was no other person in sight. It lasted only a few moments, but it was strange. A young couple then came into view across an adjacent field and the Labrador eventually turned and raced away to rejoin them.

Anyone who has experienced the loss of a much-loved family pet will know that you suddenly miss them at a myriad fleeting moments during the day – when you open the front door and expect to be wagged at or, if you're really unlucky, weed on, and you think, "You know, I wouldn't have minded that if we still had a dog". It's because they were always present, a witness and accomplice to almost every daily action, that you keep on noticing when they're not. Which all goes some way to excusing a remark my Aunty Win made many years ago as she and I sat at my dying mother's (her sister's) hospital bedside. "You know, I've had a terrible year," she said, "with Smoky the cat dying – and now there's your mother as well".

So, what amounts to a respectable period of mourning? One is surely supposed to go through a time of sorrow and respect before acquiring a "replacement". And if we did get another dog, how would it cope, labouring under the impossible burden of not being Molly?

There's no doubt that bereavement counselling has become part of the vet's job, and there are other dedicated professionals working in this field. It is clearly appreciated by clients. Margaret receives far more by way of thank you cards, flowers and chocolates from the owners of pets that she has had to put to sleep than from those that recover fully from their illness or injury. The last time the owner sees the pet will play a significant part in how they remember it; this will be the last kind thing they can do for the animal, so it is important to get it right. I have been present myself at a number of such occasions over the years and my own eyes have been known to water. I've been there when a husband and wife have arrived with an appointment for a dog to be put to sleep, having just walked him along his favourite beach for a final time. And I've watched a dog being put down at the surgery, still taking biscuits from its owner as it went under.

I read somewhere about a pet being the "social glue" that binds a family together. I make no claim for originality here – I just like the concept. I'm sure our daughter comes to visit us at weekends at least as much to see the cat as to tap us for free food and steal way with the shampoo. And our various pets over the years have proved invaluable recipients of the occasional pointed aside, "You'd think, wouldn't you, Molly, that your mother would have noticed..."

One should never underestimate the bond between the owner and even the most clapped out, flea-ridden pet. They may have been together for many years, through good times and bad, through the loss of family members. The vet has to be a good listener, and she needs to protect herself from the emotional impact, just like a doctor or nurse.

It's not just at the end but throughout the animal's life that one is dealing with both the sick pet and the owner, whatever technical expertise they may teach you on the veterinary course at university. The potentially stressful circumstances, the sometimes hushed atmosphere of the consultation, the genuine possibility that domestic changes like divorce or a death in the household may be contributing to a pet's ailment, can all prompt a client to share confidences in a way they wouldn't with their central heating engineer but might with their hairdresser. From my own experience, vets do seek to meet this need and I'm sure that Margaret and John, Sam and many, many others would agree that sensitivity comes with the territory.

Living with the b*****s, on the other hand, that's something else altogether.

But, hey, it's still been a bed of roses. I feel I must stress this. The better half has informed me on more than one occasion that she is in possession of some quite nifty drugs and some awesome looking blades and it's really, really not in my interests to complain.

It seems a pity, but I do not think I can write more

Robert Falcon Scott 1868 – 1912

Lightning Source UK Ltd.
Milton Keynes UK
UKOW07f1021121214

243057UK00012B/239/P